THE DREAM MANTLE

JEWEL ROYSTON

Understanding Mysteries Through Dreams and Visions

THE DREAM MANTLE

Volume 1: Unlocking Your Identity and Destiny

Copyright © 2022 by Jewel Royston. All rights reserved. This book or parts thereof may not be reproduced in any form stored in a retrieval system or transmitted in any form by any means – electronic, mechanical, photocopy, recording, or otherwise–without prior written permission of the publisher except as provided by the United States of America.

All Scripture is taken from the King James Version of the Bible unless otherwise noted. Public Domain.

Scriptures marked (AMP) are taken from the Amplified Bible, Copyright © 1954, 1958, 1962, 1964, 1965, 1987 by the Lockman Foundation. Used by Permission. www.Lockman.org

Scriptures marked (ERV) are taken from the Holy Bible: Easy-To-Read Version © 2001 by World Bible Translation Center, Inc. and used by permission

Scriptures marked (ESV) are taken from the ESV® Bible (The Holy Bible, English Standard Version ®), copyright © 2001 by Crossway, a publishing ministry of Good News Publishers. Used by permission.

Scripture quotations marked (NIV) are taken from the Holy Bible, New International Version®, NIV®. Copyright © 1973, 1978, 1984, 2011 by Biblica, Inc.™ Used by permission of Zondervan. All rights reserved worldwide. www.zondervan.com The "NIV" and "New International Version" are trademarks registered in the United States Patent and Trademark Office by Biblica, Inc.™

Scriptures marked (NKJV) are taken from the New King James Version®. Copyright© 1982 by Thomas Nelson, Inc. Used by permission. All rights reserved.

Scriptures marked (NLT) are taken from the Holy Bible, New Living Translation, copyright © 1996, 2004, 2007, 2013, 2015 by Tyndale House Foundation. Used by permission of Tyndale House Publishers, Inc., Carol Stream, Illinois 60188. All rights reserved.

Scriptures marked (TLB) are taken from The Living Bible copyright© 1971. Used by permission of Tyndale House Publishers, Inc., a division of Tyndale House Ministries, Carol Stream, Illinois 60188. All rights reserved.

Book cover artist: SelfPubCovers.com/RL Slather

ISBN: 978-1-952059-00-1 (paperback)

ISBN: 978-1-952059-01-8 (e-book)

Website: JewelRoyston.com

DEDICATION

I dedicate this series, *The Dream Mantle*, to my parents, David, and Margie Royston, who are also dreamers of dreams and the children of dreamers.

The secret things belong unto the LORD our God: but those things which are revealed belong unto us and to our children for ever, that we may do all the words of this law (Deuteronomy 29:29).

CONTENTS

Introduction 11

Part I: Dreams, Patterns, and Blueprints

Chapter 1 Dreams, Solutions, and Strategies 33
Chapter 2 Heavenly Patterns 39
Chapter 3 Worship, the Key to Wisdom 47
Chapter 4 Clothed in Humility 57
Chapter 5 The Mystery of Wisdom 63
Chapter 6 A Type of the King and His Kingdom 75
Chapter 7 Guard Your Heart 81

Part II: Dreams and Transfromation of The Mind

Chapter 8 Dreams and Revelatory Knowledge 87
Chapter 9 Systems 105
Chapter 10 Technology and Spiritual Capacity 113
Chapter 11 Doors in Your Mind 121
Chapter 12 Awakening to Understanding 131

Part III: The Keys

Chapter 13 The Keys of the Kingdom 143
Chapter 14 Spiritual Identity 153
Chapter 15 Revalatory Keys and Mysteries 159
Chapter 16 Mantles 163
Chapter 17 Unlocking Understanding 169
Chapter 18 Unlocking Your Destiny 181
Notes 189

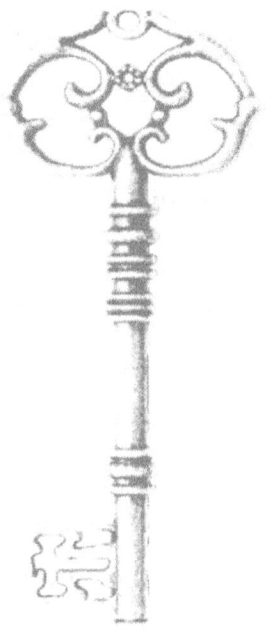

INTRODUCTION

On November 11, 2006, the Lord gave me an incredible dream that changed my life forever. It encouraged me to evaluate the health of my relationship with God and my spiritual life. I had to think about who is the Lord of my life? Who was seated on the throne of my heart, man or God? In this dream, the Lord gave me two keys representing the authority to unlock my mind (my understanding) and a path to my destiny. I have had many dreams about keys, but they do not always look like door keys. However, they have the same function: authority to open doors to wisdom, understanding, and knowledge. These keys can also access heavenly realms containing the mysteries or secret things of God. God can use dreams the same way a professor uses a PowerPoint presentation to help the student focus on the most important information he wants his students to remember. God uses dreams to teach us humility, how to hear His voice, impart wisdom, release instructions, transform our minds, give warnings and discernment. Dreams can also reveal God's will for our lives.

Spiritual dreams are a gateway to understanding mysteries. They are an intimate form of communication that reveal God's heart and mind concerning His divine will and purpose for our lives. They are not just prophetic—reflections of the future; they can also be reflections of the present and the past. You may have struggled to understand the application of your dreams until the Lord unlocked understanding and wisdom concerning those dreams.

Spiritual dreams are also projections of what presently exist in the spiritual or unseen realm. They can illustrate the authority given unto us as believers to establish God's order in the earth realm. All dreams have a purpose, but God does not inspire all dreams. Dreams can reflect what is going on in the mind and heart because of sleep deprivation or stressful situations created by a hostile environment. One of the best ways to determine if God has inspired a dream is by researching Scriptures that may support or illustrate the dream's message. Dreams inspired by the Spirit of God will not contradict the Scriptures, God's character, or God's will. Some people believe some dreams are a response to what we have eaten and call those pizza dreams. Dreams can be a response to what has been planted in our hearts and minds. Sometimes what a person has watched, meditated on, or talked about can become the star of a dream.

NAVIGATING THE DREAM REALM

The senses we use to interact with the environment to differentiate one experience, color, taste, texture, or smell from another help us to understand our dreams. For example, our vision can become like the zoom lens on a camera, though we may be nearsighted. What our eyes focus on helps us to identify the most important elements in the dream. In the dream realm, our senses can unlock different dimensions of discernment. "Discernment is the act of discerning; also, the power or faculty of the mind, by which it distinguishes one thing from another, as truth from falsehood, virtue from vice; acuteness of judgment; power of perceiving differences of things or ideas, and their relations and tendencies."

There are many different types of dreams. Some dreams are designed to deliver us from oppressive environmental and cultural systems developed by unhealthy belief systems. Other dreams can reveal the transformation that God wants to bring to the Church and the world.

SOULISH DREAMS

Dreams inspired by our senses or external influences and not by the Holy Spirit are soulish dreams. They are manufactured by the soul: the mind, will, emotions, and intellect. One of the purposes of these dreams is to help the mind bring order to the day's events that may have been emotionally or physically exhausting. The mind, specifically the subconscious mind, can also be impacted through our dreams to help us adapt to changing situations and environments.

SEXUAL DREAMS

Sexual dreams are a type of soulish dream. God is not the producer nor director of these dreams. However, these dreams have a purpose and can help us recognize the need to receive inner healing and deliverance from unresolved issues related to abusive or traumatic experiences. These types of dreams can also be produced by what we watch and listen to via different forms of media.

DEMONIC DREAMS

Dreams inspired by external influences such as ungodly spirits are demonic dreams. We sometimes encounter these entities while we sleep and when we are awake because they are a part of the spiritual realm. Demonic spirits can invade our dreams when we engage in ungodly practices such as psychic readings. Traumatic experiences can also produce demonic dreams that may require inner healing and deliverance ministry in addition to professional counseling. "For our struggle is not against flesh and blood [contending only with physical opponents], but against the rulers, against the powers, against the world forces of this [present] darkness, against the spiritual *forces* of wickedness in the heavenly (supernatural) *places*" (Ephesians 6:12 AMP).

FALSE DREAMS

Unlike soulish dreams, false dreams are fabricated, contrived, or made up from the imagination. In the Bible, they were birthed out of the hearts of false prophets. False dreams are designed to lead people away from God and the Word of God through false teachings.

> This is what the LORD All-Powerful says: "Don't pay attention to what those prophets are saying to you. They are trying to fool you. They talk about visions, but they did not get their visions from me. Their visions come from their own minds. I am against the false prophets who tell false dreams." This message is from the LORD. "They mislead my people with their lies and false teachings. I did not send them to teach the people. I never commanded them to do anything for me..." (Jeremiah 23:16, 32 ERV)

Always refer to the Bible to verify that the integrity of God's Word is being maintained in a dream's message and interpretation. I have heard people say the test of a true prophet is that what he says comes to pass. A person can have dreams that come to pass and be in error concerning biblical doctrine. The person's inspiration may not be from the Holy Spirit. "If a prophet, or one who foretells by dreams, appears among you and announces to you a sign or wonder, and if the sign or wonder spoken of takes place, and the prophet says, 'Let us follow other gods' (gods you have not known) 'and let us worship them,' you must not listen to the words of that prophet or dreamer. The LORD your God is testing you to find out whether you love him with all your heart and with all your soul" (Deuteronomy 13:1–3 NIV).

Today there is a great interest in dreams and misinterpreted dreams are being shared on social media concerning the sign of the times. Dreams must be carefully judged with the Word of God, and we must be sensitive to the Holy Spirit to know when to release a dream at the appropriate time. Dreams reflecting the sign of the times are designed to help people prepare themselves for changes in the world's systems.

Dreams can be illustrations of Scriptures. They can help us unlock mysteries hidden in the Word of God. However, our primary source of revelation should come from the Bible and the Holy Spirit. "And so we have the prophetic word confirmed, which you do well to heed as a light that shines in a dark place, until the day dawns and the morning star rises in your hearts; knowing this first, that no prophecy of Scripture is of any private interpretation, for prophecy never came by the will of man, but holy men of God spoke as they were moved by the Holy Spirit" (2 Peter 1:19–21 NKJV).

The purpose of this book is to help you understand how to unlock your spiritual identity, destiny, and potential with the knowledge communicated in dreams. Spiritual dreams have the power to influence our thoughts, desires, and priorities to come into alignment with God's will for our lives. God is a Spirit, and he speaks to our spirit even when we sleep. When God speaks to us in our dreams, His words are so powerful; they can leave an impression on our soul that changes unhealthy thought patterns and belief systems. Spiritual dreams are one of many ways the Lord uses to creatively reveal information to us to unlock our spiritual and intellectual capacity.

MYSTERIES

The day I began rewriting this book, the Lord spoke to me and said, "It has been given unto you to know the mysteries of the kingdom." I felt the Lord download or drop something into my spirit as he spoke. God had answered my prayer: "Lord, give me a spirit of understanding." There is a word that describes my experience: nataph. According to the *Strong's Exhaustive Concordance*, nataph means, distil gradually; by implication, to fall in drops; figuratively, to speak by inspiration, dropping–prophecy. Moses gave us an analogy that describes how we can receive a revelation, like how the rain gently falls to nourish and help plants grow. "Give ear, O heavens, and I will speak; And hear, O earth, the words of my mouth. Let my teaching drop as the rain, My speech distill as the dew, As raindrops on the tender herb, And as showers on the grass. For I proclaim the name of the Lord: Ascribe greatness to our God" (Deuteronomy 32:1–3 NKJV).

According to *Vine's Complete Expository Dictionary of Old and New Testament Words*, mystery is defined as "being outside the range of unassisted natural apprehension, can be made known only by divine revelation, and is made known in a manner and at the time appointed by God, and to those only who are illuminated by His Spirit. In the ordinary sense, a 'mystery' implies knowledge withheld; its Scriptural significance is truth revealed."

Jesus told the disciples they were permitted to understand the mysteries of the kingdom of heaven. He also said to them that whoever listened to His teachings about the kingdom of heaven would receive more. The disciples would receive more revelation and access to what exists in the kingdom of heaven—wisdom, understanding, knowledge, power, authority, divine patterns, and blueprints.

> Then the disciples came to Him and asked, "Why do You speak to the crowds in parables?" Jesus replied to them, "To you it has been granted to know the mysteries of the kingdom of heaven, but to them it has not been granted. For whoever has [spiritual wisdom because he is receptive to God's word], to him more will be given, and he will be richly *and* abundantly supplied; but whoever does not have [spiritual wisdom because he has devalued God's word], even what he has will be taken away from him. (Matthew 13:10–12 AMP)

Our relationship with the Lord is not only influenced by our knowledge base of Scriptures but by the time we spend in prayer seeking instructions and directions. God reveals His secrets to transform our minds and release our potential. The secret things revealed to us become a part of our families' spiritual inheritance. Deuteronomy 29:29 states, "The secret things belong unto the Lord our God: but those things which are revealed belong unto us and to our children for ever, that we may do all the words of this law."

There is a direct correlation between our obedience, the intimacy we have in our relationship with the Lord, and the amount of revelation we can receive. Secrets are revealed to those who reverence and honor the Lord. "The secret [of the wise counsel] of the LORD is for those who fear

Him, And He will let them know His covenant *and* reveal to them [through His word] its [deep, inner] meaning" (Psalm 25:14 AMP).

PARABLE OF THE LAMP

In the parable of the lamp, Jesus reiterates the more His disciples listened to His teaching, the more insight would be given to them. Insight is "the capacity to gain an accurate and deep understanding of a person or thing." In the parable of the lamp, Jesus expounded on how mysteries—hidden or secret things exist to be revealed to those who are teachable. He also explained that the value the disciples placed on the Word of God and how they applied it would determine how much more insight would be given. According to *The Prophet's Dictionary*, a lamp symbolizes enlightenment, instruction, and guidance. The parable of the lamp illustrates that enlightenment, instruction, and guidance, hidden in the Word of God exist to be revealed.

> He said to them, "A lamp is not brought in to be put under a basket or under a bed, is it? Is it not [brought in] to be put on the lampstand? For nothing is hidden, except to be revealed; nor has anything been kept secret, but that it would come to light [that is, things are hidden only temporarily, until the appropriate time comes for them to be known]. If anyone has ears to hear, let him hear *and* heed My words." Then He said to them, "Pay attention to what you hear. By your own standard of measurement [that is, to the extent that you study spiritual truth and apply godly wisdom] it will be measured to you [and you

will be given even greater ability to respond]—and *more* will be given to you besides. For whoever has [a teachable heart], to him more [understanding] will be given; and whoever does not have [a yearning for truth], even what he has will be taken away from him." (Mark 4:21–25 AMP)

DIVINE COMMUNICATION

In the Old Testament, God spoke through dreams and visions to prophets and those he placed in authority. God spoke to Moses face to face and not in riddles. Riddles, like dreams, require interpretation. God rebuked Miriam and Aaron for criticizing Moses. The Lord had placed Moses in a higher position of authority than the prophets among them. God spoke to him face to face because he trusted Moses. The type of relationship we have with God determines how he speaks to us. Our relationship with God influences the amount of authority and responsibility given to us. God said Moses "sees the Lord as he is" (Numbers 12:8 NLT), meaning Moses understood the heart and will of God.

> Then the Lord descended in the pillar of cloud and stood at the entrance of the Tabernacle. "Aaron and Miriam!" he called, and they stepped forward. And the Lord said to them, "Now listen to what I say: "If there were prophets among you, I, the Lord, would reveal myself in visions. I would speak to them in dreams. But not with my servant Moses. Of all my house, he is the one I trust. I speak to him face to face, clearly, and not in riddles!

He sees the Lord as he is. So why were you not afraid to criticize my servant Moses?" (Numbers 12:5–8 NLT)

Let's talk about the importance of being able to understand riddles. A riddle is "a statement, question or phrase having a double or veiled meaning, put forth as a puzzle to be solved. Riddles are of two types: *enigmas*, which are problems generally expressed in metaphorical or allegorical language that requires ingenuity and careful thinking for their solution, and *conundra*, which are questions relying for their effects on punning in either the question or the answer."

When King Belshazzar, the son of King Nebuchadnezzar, had a banquet for nobles, he decided to allow the nobles, his wives, and concubines to drink out of the cups that his father had taken out of the temple of God in Jerusalem. A hand appeared and wrote a message on the wall. He called for the wise men to interpret the writing, but they could not interpret it (see Daniel 5:1–10). The queen informed the king that a man (Daniel) in his kingdom had a spirit of knowledge, understanding, and wisdom. He could interpret dreams, clarify riddles, and solve complex problems.

> There is a man in your kingdom in whom is a spirit of the holy gods; and in the days of your father, illumination, understanding and wisdom like the wisdom of the gods were found in him. And King Nebuchadnezzar, your father—your father the king, appointed him chief of the magicians, enchanters, Chaldeans and diviners. It was because an extraordinary spirit, knowledge and insight, the ability to interpret dreams, clarify riddles, and solve complex problems were found in this Daniel, whom the king named

Belteshazzar. Now let Daniel be called and he will give the interpretation. (Daniel 5:11–12 AMP)

Kings and government officials have received guidance and instructions through dreams throughout the Bible. King Saul received God's guidance through dreams and messages spoken through prophets. When he saw the enemies of Israel mobilizing, he needed instructions from God. Because of Saul's previous disobedience to God's instructions in conquering Israel's enemies, all communication from God ceased. The following Scriptures suggest God gave Saul strategies not only by casting lots and prophets but by dreams to defeat his enemies and advance the kingdom of God. "The Philistines set up their camp at Shunem, and Saul gathered all the army of Israel and camped at Gilboa. When Saul saw the vast Philistine army, he became frantic with fear. He asked the LORD what he should do, but the LORD refused to answer him, either by dreams or by sacred lots or by the prophets" (1 Samuel 28:4–6 NLT).

According to the article, "What Is Casting Lots?," "Casting lots was a method used by the Jews of the Old Testament and by the Christian disciples prior to Pentecost to determine the will of God. Lots could be sticks with markings, stones with symbols, etc., which were thrown into a small area, and then the result was interpreted." The article cites the following Scripture: "The lot is cast into the lap, but it's every decision is from the LORD" (Proverbs 16:33 AMP). Note that the article states that the method of casting of lots was used prior to Pentecost—the outpouring of the Holy Spirit on God's people to empower them.

Instead of repenting, Saul asked his advisers to send for the witch of Endor so she could conjure up the dead Prophet Samuel's spirit. He desired to receive counsel from the spirit of the dead Prophet Samuel. Communication with the dead is necromancy, and it is very dangerous to consult with mediums.

> Saul then said to his advisers, "Find a woman who is a medium, so I can go and ask her what to do." His advisers replied, "There is a medium at Endor." So Saul disguised himself by wearing ordinary clothing instead of his royal robes. Then he went to the woman's home at night, accompanied by two of his men. "I have to talk to a man who has died," he said. "Will you call up his spirit for me?" Finally the woman said, "Whom shall I call up?" "Call up Samuel," Saul replied. (1 Samuel 28:7–8, 11 NLT)

Unfortunately, today's mediums are highly sought after, have television shows, and have written many books. However, the Bible expressly forbids consulting with mediums, fortune tellers, or partaking in necromancy. These practices are also a door to the occult. "The word 'occult' comes from a Latin word for 'hidden.' It is a collection of beliefs and practices founded on the premise that humans can tap into a supernatural world. Once connected to this other realm, various rituals and special knowledge are used by those involved in the occult to allow a person to gain abilities and power they would otherwise not possess." As the children of God, if we need direction, we should seek to hear God's voice through prayer and reading the Bible. Look at the following Scriptures forbidding consulting with mediums, fortune tellers, or necromancers.

Give no regard to mediums and familiar spirits; do not seek after them, to be defiled by them: I *am* the LORD your God. (Leviticus 19:31 NKJV)

And when they say to you, "Seek those who are mediums and wizards, who whisper and mutter," should not a people seek their God? *Should they seek* the dead on behalf of the living? (Isaiah 8:19 NKJV)

"When you come into the land which the LORD your God is giving you, you shall not learn to follow the abominations of those nations There shall not be found among you *anyone* who makes his son or his daughter pass through the fire, *or one* who practices witchcraft, *or* a soothsayer, or one who interprets omens, or a sorcerer, or one who conjures spells, or a medium, or a spiritist, or one who calls up the dead. For all who do these things *are* an abomination to the LORD, and because of these abominations the LORD your God..." (Deuteronomy 18:9–12 NKJV)

A SHIFT IN DIVINE COMMUNICATION

We see a shift in whom God will speak to in the New Testament. He primarily spoke to prophets and those he placed in authority in the Old Testament, such as kings. The Prophet Joel prophesied that God would pour out His Spirit on all flesh in the last days. The outpouring of His Spirit would result in prophecy, dreams, and visions, not just for those with governmental authority.

In the beginning, God used visions and dreams to communicate to humanity, and in the last days, the days we are living in, God will continue to speak to us this way. Joel's prophecy identifies the beginning of the last days and the empowering of people through the outpouring of the Holy Spirit. "'It shall come about after this That I shall pour out My Spirit on all mankind; And your sons and your daughters will prophesy, Your old men will dream dreams, Your young men will see visions. 'Even on the male and female servants I will pour out My Spirit in those days'" (Joel 2:28–29 AMP).

The Apostle Peter received a revelation; the upper room experience was the beginning of Joel's prophecy coming to pass. He cleverly said, "But *this is that* which was spoken by the prophet Joel" (Acts 2:16, emphasis added). Peter also explained this experience as the fulfillment of Jesus's promise to send the disciples another Comforter, the Holy Spirit. Jesus instructed the disciples to wait in the upper room for the Holy Spirit. The Scriptures reveal that God had given Jesus authority to send the Holy Spirit to the disciples. "'And now he sits on the throne of highest honor in heaven, next to God. And just as promised, the Father gave him the authority to send the Holy Spirit—with the results you are seeing and hearing today'" (Acts 2:33 TLB).

DREAM ENCOUNTERS

Encounters with the presence of God can unlock dreams, visions, power, authority, different types of anointings, purpose, God-ordained assignments, your spiritual identity, and destiny. A dream encounter is an unexpected meeting in the spiritual realm designed to awaken you, change your thought patterns, and the course of your life to conform with the will of God. God opened a gate to the spiritual realm through dreams for Jacob. In Jacob's first dream, a ladder with the top reaching heaven as angels traveled back and forth between heaven and earth appeared. God was at the top of this ladder. God revealed another dimension of his identity to Jacob, the Lord God of Abraham, his grandfather, and the God of Isaac, his father. "He dreamed that there was a ladder (stairway) placed on the earth, and the top of it reached [out of sight] toward heaven; and [he saw] the angels of God ascending and descending on it [going to and from heaven]. And behold, the Lord stood above and around him and said, 'I am the LORD, the God of Abraham your [father's] father and the God of Isaac; I will give to you and to your descendants the land [of promise] on which you are lying'" (Genesis 28:12–13 AMP).

Jacob experienced a physical and spiritual awakening. God gave Jacob a revelation of the gate to the kingdom of heaven and the ministry of angels to humanity. The gate represents access to the presence of God by a revelation or revelatory knowledge released to him in his dream, referred to as Jacob's Ladder. However, Jacob's most significant revelation was acknowledging God as the Lord and God of his fathers; God unlocked Jacob's legacy. "Then Jacob awoke from his sleep and he said, 'Without any doubt the LORD is in this place, and I did not realize it.' So he was afraid and said, 'How fearful *and* awesome is this place! This is none other than the house of God, and this is the gateway to heaven'" (Genesis 28:16–17 AMP).

Sometimes our struggles in life reveal our God-given strength. In another encounter, Jacob unknowingly wrestled with God. His wrestling caused him to engage in close contact (intimacy) with God. Intimacy with God unlocks our understanding of different dimensions of God's identity and our own. When he stopped struggling with God, God blessed him and revealed that he had received power, authority, and a new name. Jacob was given power with God and man. He received authority in two different realms: heaven and earth. Authority determines where the power that has been given to a person can be exercised. "Your name shall no longer be called Jacob, but Israel; for you have struggled with God and with men, and have prevailed" So Jacob called the name of the place Peniel: 'For I have seen God face to face, and my life is preserved'" (Genesis 32:28, 30 NKJV).

Our encounters with God's presence, even in dreams, have the power to transform our hearts and minds. Dream encounters with God's presence can train us to discern God's Spirit from other spirits. They can also teach us to recognize the voice of God inside and outside of the dream realm. The connection we have to the Spirit of God when we are awake is continually active even when we sleep. God desires to commune with us continually.

> If I ride the wings of the morning, if I dwell by the farthest oceans, even there your hand will guide me, and your strength will support me. I could ask the darkness to hide me and the light around me to become night—but even in darkness I cannot

hide from you. To you the night shines as bright as day. Darkness and light are the same to you. How precious are your thoughts about me, O God. They cannot be numbered! I can't even count them; they outnumber the grains of sand! And when I wake up, you are still with me! (Psalms 139:9–12, 17–18 NLT)

ASSIGNMENTS, DREAMS, AND VISIONS

When Saul of Tarsus was on the road to Damascus, he had an encounter with Jesus. He received a revelation of who Jesus is. "As he was approaching Damascus on this mission, a light from heaven suddenly shone down around him. He fell to the ground and heard a voice saying to him, 'Saul! Saul! Why are you persecuting me?' 'Who are you, lord?' Saul asked. And the voice replied, 'I am Jesus, the one you are persecuting!'" (Acts 9:3–5 NLT). Saul received a revelation that his persecution of the Church, the body of Christ, was the same as persecuting Jesus. Saul's encounter was the beginning of his conversion and transformation (see Acts 9:6–20).

Saul's encounter with the presence of God unlocked his spiritual identity and destiny. He would no longer be known as Saul; he would become known as Paul, the apostle, who was full of the Holy Spirit (see Acts 13:9). Full of the Spirit of God, Paul could write about the mysteries of God. The Lord gave Paul insight concerning wisdom, understanding, and knowledge.

As we take this journey into the supernatural realm by exploring dreams and visions, the Holy Spirit and the Scriptures must be our guides. No matter our title, position, or status, we can have an encounter with God designed to unlock the authority and power that He delegates to us as believers. God gives us insight into dreams that has the power to awaken us to our purpose and identity in the kingdom.

PART I

DREAMS, PATTERNS, AND BLUEPRINTS

CHAPTER 1
DREAMS, SOLUTIONS, AND STRATEGIES

God can give us wisdom, understanding, knowledge, directions, instructions, and solutions to our problems in our dreams to guide us in our daily lives. Dreams can help us unlock our identity and destiny. Jacob went to his uncle Laban's family when he desired to be married. He fell in love with his uncle's daughter, Rachel. Jacob agreed to work for his uncle for seven years to marry Rachel. Laban not only tricked him into marrying his oldest daughter, but he made Jacob work an additional seven years before he could marry Rachel. God used a dream to deliver Jacob from his uncle's schemes and more importantly, to instruct him to return home to establish his legacy. In the dream, God sent an angel to Jacob; the angel revealed a strategy to Jacob that made him wealthy. Jacob received another revelation of who God is (the God he met at Bethel) and the ministry of angels (see Genesis 31:6–13).

DREAMS THAT UNLOCK IDENTITY AND DESTINY

Another example of how God uses dreams to reveal strategies that unlock one's identity and destiny is illustrated in the story of Joseph in Egypt. The King of Egypt had two dreams that troubled him, so he sent for the magicians and wise men to interpret his dreams. When they could not interpret the dreams, Pharoah's chief butler, who had spent time in prison with Joseph, testified to Pharoah about Joseph's gift to interpret dreams. The chief butler's testimony signified that there is an appointed time for our identity and destiny to be unlocked (see Genesis 41:8–13).

God had been preparing Joseph for many years for a position of power in the Kingdom of Egypt. God would use the mantle (the anointing, authority, and position) He had given Joseph to navigate the dream realm. He had been anointed to provide solutions and strategies for systemic problems through his ability to interpret dreams and visions.

Pharoah immediately sent for Joseph. Joseph made himself presentable and changed his clothes. Prophetically, Joseph changing his clothes signified that his anointing, authority, and position had changed. He would no longer be the servant to the captain of the guard in prison. When Joseph encountered Pharaoh, Pharoah said to Joseph he was told that when he heard a dream, he could interpret it. Joseph humbly told Pharoah that the wisdom to interpret dreams comes from God (the Holy Spirit) and not from him (his intellect). "'It is not in me [to interpret the dream]; God [not I] will give Pharaoh a favorable answer [through me]'" (Genesis 41:16 AMP).

Pharaoh told Joseph his two dreams. In the first dream, he dreamt of seven fat cows coming out of a river. Then, seven lean cows appeared and consumed the seven fat cows. In his second dream, he saw seven unhealthy ears of corn on one stalk, devouring seven healthy ears of corn on one stalk. Did you notice that symbols that would point to the solution and plan to survive the famine came out of a river? In dreams, a river can represent the Holy Spirit, the Word of God, and life. The King of Egypt would receive revelation to save many lives (see Genesis 41:17–24).

THE MYSTERY OF THE DOUBLE DREAM

All of Egypt was moving toward a time of famine; God gave the King of Egypt a double dream, two different dreams that carried the same message. Joseph explained to Pharoah that the healthy cows and ears of corn represented seven years of abundance while the unhealthy cows and ears of corn represented seven years of famine. God revealed the mystery of a double dream to Joseph. The double dream confirmed that what God had already established in heaven would quickly come to pass in the earth realm (see Genesis 41:25–32).

Some dreams are illustrations of the gifts of the Holy Spirit, which are listed in 1 Corinthians 12:4–11. Pharaoh's dream is an illustration of the word of wisdom. According to the study course series titled *The Holy Spirit and His Gifts*, "The word of wisdom is a supernatural revelation by the Spirit of God concerning the divine purpose and plan in the mind and will of God."

The interpretation of the double dream enabled Joseph to develop a strategy and a solution to overcome the time of famine in the Kingdom of Egypt and all other countries. He developed a system to distribute the grain. Joseph also gave Pharaoh instructions for specific storage locations for the grain. Today these storage places are known as the Joseph Storehouses. When I went to Egypt in 2019, I visited these storehouses. We saw the technology used in Joseph's time and how well organized the early Egyptian civilization was as we walked through the different stations of the granaries. Our tour guide is an Egyptologist that works with a university in Egypt. He has in-depth knowledge of Egyptian agriculture and the irrigation systems used in Joseph's time. We also were able to see the water source for the irrigation system that was used. We learned a lot of historical information revealed through the continual archeological digs that support the Bible's account of Joseph's time in Egypt (see Genesis 41:33–36).

The value placed on dreams in the Egyptian culture would explain the King of Egypt embracing a strategy birthed out of a dream to save Egypt from famine. According to an article titled, "Perchance to Dream," dreams are an important part of Egyptian culture. The Egyptians received dreams as divine guidance and direction. "The 'New Age' subject of dream interpretation isn't new at all. Thousands of years ago, ancient Egyptians used the messages in their dreams in order to cure illnesses, make important State decisions, and even to decide where to build a temple or when to wage a battle. Dreams were considered to be divine predictions of the future."

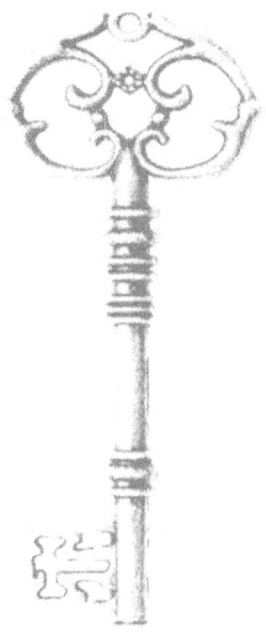

CHAPTER 2
HEAVENLY PATTERNS

Patterns in the Bible illustrate the order of the kingdom of heaven. These patterns are illustrated in systems of worship, prayers, dreams, and visions. Examples of heavenly patterns to help us understand God's will and order include the Tabernacle of Moses, the Lord's prayer, and King Solomon's dream. Heavenly patterns are to be followed from generation to generation. However, some patterns like the Old Testament pattern of worship had to be replaced to give the people greater access to God's presence without the priest's ceremonial duties, which prepared only the priest to enter the temple on behalf of the people. They would perform these rituals annually to atone for the people's sins and restore a right relationship between God and the people (see Hebrews 9:6–10).

THE WORSHIP PATTERN

When Moses spent time communing with God on Mount Sinai, he was given a pattern for a system of worship and an assignment to design it after the one in heaven. The Tabernacle of Moses was a mobile worship system and is a type and a shadow, pointing us to a New Testament system of worship. In this new system of worship, Jesus is our High Priest. As our High Priest, Jesus has given us access to God the Father and the kingdom of heaven.

> Here is the main point: We have a High Priest who sat down in the place of honor beside the throne of the majestic God in heaven. There he ministers in the heavenly Tabernacle, the true place of worship that was built by the Lord and not by human hands. And since every high priest is required to offer gifts and sacrifices, our High Priest must make an offering, too. If he were here on earth, he would not even be a priest, since there already are priests who offer the gifts required by the law. They serve in a system of worship that is only a copy, a shadow of the real one in heaven. For when Moses was getting ready to build the Tabernacle, God gave him this warning: "Be sure that you

make everything according to the pattern I have shown you here on the mountain." (Hebrews 8:1–5 NLT)

THE MODEL PRAYER PATTERN

The Lord's Prayer is sometimes referred to as the model prayer because it teaches us a pattern of how to pray. It gives us instructions concerning whom we should direct our prayers to ("Our Father, which art in heaven") and what we should pray about ("Thy kingdom come, Thy will be done on earth, as it is in heaven"). The Lord's Prayer highlights that we should pray for the kingdom to come. We are praying for God's order and will to be manifested, not a physical kingdom. The kingdom of God exists in the spiritual realm. This prayer pattern was revealed when the disciples asked Jesus to teach them how to pray. "After this manner therefore pray ye: Our Father which art in heaven, Hallowed be thy name. Thy kingdom come, Thy will be done in earth, as it is in heaven. Give us this day our daily bread. And forgive us our debts, as we forgive our debtors. And lead us not into temptation, but deliver us from evil: For thine is the kingdom, and the power, and the glory, for ever. Amen" (Matthew 6:9–13).

THE DREAM PATTERN

I will use Solomon's dream to explain how God uses dreams to impart wisdom, understanding, and knowledge. Worship initiated Solomon's encounter with the Lord. God increased Solomon's spiritual capacity by downloading information into his spirit in this encounter. The information he received also transformed his mind. Worship transforms our hearts, and the Word of God renews our minds. Dreams can affect us subconsciously to change our innermost desires and thoughts. "'For God speaks again and again, in dreams, in visions of the night when deep sleep falls on men as they lie on their beds. He opens their ears in times like that and gives them wisdom and instruction, causing them to change their minds, and keeping them from pride, and warning them of the penalties of sin, and keeping them from falling into some trap'" (Job 33:14–18 TLB).

In the previous passage, God reveals seven of many things that he can impart to us while we dream. We can see that the first five things mentioned in Job 33:44–18 are illustrated in King Solomon's dream. God used revelatory knowledge to impart these things to Solomon.

1. An ability to hear the voice of God
2. Wisdom
3. Instructions
4. Transformation of the mind
5. Humility
6. Warnings about the consequence of sin
7. Discernment

In examining Solomon's dream encounter with God, we see a pattern and a door to wisdom open. He worshipped the Lord and the Lord appeared to him in a dream. Worship prepares our hearts and minds to receive the Word of God. Worship is the key that opens the door, not just to wisdom but to the presence of God.

Solomon loved the LORD…offered sacrifices and burned incense at the local places of worship. The most important of these places of worship was at Gibeon, so the king went there and sacrificed 1,000 burnt offerings. That night the Lord appeared to Solomon in a dream, and God said, "What do you want?" "Ask, and I will give it to you!" "Now, O Lord my God, you have made me king instead of my father, David, but I am like a little child who doesn't know his way around. And here I am in the midst of your own chosen people, a nation so great and numerous they cannot be counted! Give me an understanding heart so that I can govern your people well and know the difference between right and wrong. For who by himself is able to govern this great people of yours?" So God replied "Because you have asked for wisdom in governing my people with justice…I will give you a wise and understanding heart such as no one else has had or ever will have!" Then Solomon woke up and realized it had been a dream…(1 Kings 3:3–5, 7, 9, 11–12, 15 NLT)

Note that Solomon asked for an understanding heart in the above passage of Scriptures, and God revealed to Solomon that he was asking for wisdom to rule with justice. One definition of wisdom is "the ability to discern inner qualities and relationships or insight." Understanding is defined: 1.) a mental grasp or comprehension 2.) the power of comprehending, especially the capacity to apprehend general relations of particulars.

DREAMS AND OUR BELIEF SYSTEM

King Solomon's dream changed his perception of his ability to rule the kingdom. In the dream, he poured out his heart's deepest desires before the Lord concerning how to govern the kingdom. Solomon loved and worshipped the Lord. The greater the degree of intimacy we have in our relationship with the Lord, the greater our access to wisdom, understanding, and revelatory knowledge. Interestingly, King Solomon's request in his dream encounter with the Lord is a reflection of the Lord's Prayer. He asked for God's will and order to be established on earth through the kingdom he would rule.

In our dreams, we can receive a revelation of spiritual gifts and different types of anointing that will be imparted to complete a God-given assignment. In Solomon's dream, God said He would give Solomon wisdom by giving him a wise and understanding heart to rule the kingdom. When God says He would give Solomon a wise and understanding heart, He was inferring that He would increase Solomon's spiritual and mental capacity.

Did you notice that what Solomon believed in his heart, he also believed in his dream? He knew God continually shows love to those who are honest and faithful. Did you also notice that Solomon's dream required very little analysis or interpretation? God had explained to Solomon what he was asking for in his dream. What we believe and understand, we carry into the dream realm. However, when our belief systems need to be transformed, and our understanding elevated, God can give us a revelation to change how we think. The Lord changed Solomon's capacity for understanding. Now, he could understand and live out in reality what he did not previously understand. According to *Webster's New World Dictionary of the American Language*, capacity is "the power of receiving and holding knowledge, impressions, etc.; mental ability." The information released to us in dreams can increase our spiritual capacity to understand mysteries.

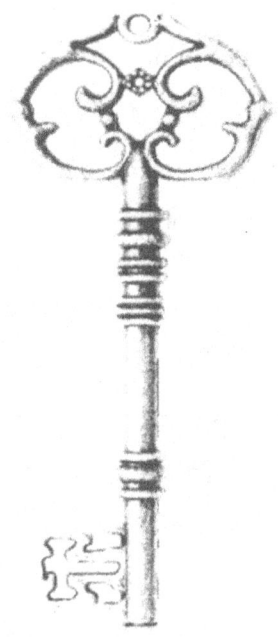

CHAPTER 3
WORSHIP, THE KEY TO WISDOM

King Solomon's quest for wisdom began with worship. Worship is adoration or an expression of love that we have for God. The more time we spend in communion with God, the more we can understand the heart and will of God. Worship is a way to learn how to hear the voice of God. It does not necessarily require words. Worship is communication between your spirit and the Spirit of God. We worship God with our love and obedience. However, King Solomon offered animal sacrifices as a part of his worship to express his love for God, and the Lord responded in King Solomon's dream that night. The two had an amazing dialogue about the wisdom, understanding, and knowledge that would be imparted to him. Worship is communion and communication; an essential part of worship is listening. Once we have expressed our adoration to the Lord, we should enter into a place of silence and being still so the Lord can speak to us. In this place of silence, we can unlock God's purpose and will for our lives.

WORSHIP AND THE MINISTRY OF THE SCRIBES

In the Bible, some priests did not only conduct worship services; they were assigned to record events and the writings of kings. They were known as scribes and played an important role in recording Israel's history. As scribes, the priests helped preserve what we know about worship and access to the presence of God. The book titled, *The Tabernacle of David* states: "King David set Levites in his Tabernacle to record. It involved the ministry of the scribe. Many of the Psalms, especially those which concern Zion, must have been given by the inspiration of the Holy Spirit in connection to the Tabernacle of David…The Psalms would be recorded by the Levitical scribes and thus set down so they could be remembered… Moses was the only one who wrote inspired Scripture in relation to the Tabernacle called by his name. Psalms 90–91 have been attributed to Moses."

The Psalms help us unlock revelation in the Scriptures concerning the presence of God. They also help us understand the power of prayer, praise, and worship so that God's presence can become our habitation.

God's presence is our "dwelling place" or "shelter" is expressed in the Psalms attributed to Moses. Look at the following Scriptures in the book of Psalms that have been attributed to Moses:

> Lord, You have been our dwelling place [our refuge, our sanctuary, our stability] in all generations. (Psalm 90:1 AMP)

> He who dwells in the shelter of the Most High Will remain secure *and* rest in the shadow of the Almighty [whose power no enemy can withstand]. I will say of the LORD, "He is my refuge and my fortress, My God, in whom I trust [with great confidence, and on whom I rely]!" For He will save you from the trap of the fowler, And from the deadly pestilence. He will cover you *and* completely protect you with His pinions, And under His wings you will find refuge; His faithfulness is a shield and a wall. Because you have made the LORD, [who is] my refuge, Even the Most-High, your dwelling place, No evil will befall you, Nor will any plague come near your tent. (Psalm 91:1–4, 9–10 AMP)

THE MOSAIC AND DAVIDIC PROTOTYPE

Moses and King David were given divine patterns and instructions for building a place for God's presence to commune with Israel. We see a paradigm shift when we look at how Moses, King David, and King Solomon worshipped. Worship evolves from building tabernacles to building the first temple. Before Solomon had his dream encounter with the Lord, he went to Gibeon, where Moses had built the tabernacle or the

Tent of Meeting. 2 Chronicles 1:5 documents that Solomon and the congregation sought for this place where the presence of God had communed with Israel. They worshipped at the altar built in Moses's time. 2 Chronicles 1 gives us a more detailed second account of what preceded Solomon's dream encounter with the Lord.

> And Solomon, and all the assembly with him, went to the high place that was at Gibeon, for the tent of meeting of God, which Moses the servant of the LORD had made in the wilderness, was there. (But David had brought up the ark of God from Kiriath-jearim to the place that David had prepared for it, for he had pitched a tent for it in Jerusalem.) Moreover, the bronze altar that Bezalel the son of Uri, son of Hur, had made, was there before the Tabernacle of the LORD. And Solomon and the assembly sought it out. And Solomon went up there to the bronze altar before the LORD, which was at the tent of meeting, and offered a thousand burnt offerings on it. In that night God appeared to Solomon, and said to him, "Ask what I shall give you." (2 Chronicles 1:3–7 ESV)

THE TEMPLE OF SOLOMON

King David desired to build a house for the presence of God, but God had given this assignment to his son Solomon. David received the blueprints for the Temple of God from the Holy Spirit. Before David gave Solomon the blueprints, he gave Solomon instructions to continue ruling the kingdom and establishing his legacy. David's understanding of the importance of worship, the condition of the heart, and mind enabled him to give Solomon wise counsel (see 1 Chronicles 28:8–12).

THE HEART AND MIND OF A WORSHIPPER

We can see the importance God has placed on one's heart when the Prophet Samuel was sent to anoint one of Jesse's sons as King of Israel. He found David among his brothers, who appeared to be more suitable as king than David because of their physical appearance of having strength. Samuel did not know that God had chosen David because of his heart. "But the LORD said to Samuel, 'Do not look at his appearance or at his physical stature, because I have refused him. For *the LORD does not see as man sees*; for man looks at the outward appearance, but the LORD looks at the heart'" (1 Samuel 16:7 NKJV, emphasis added).

THE BLUEPRINT

When David released the blueprint to Solomon to build the Temple of God, he told Solomon, do not be discouraged by the assignment or the task's size. He informed Solomon that he would have divine help in completing the assignment. David had received revelatory knowledge from the Holy Spirit to design the Temple of God. Solomon would have to follow every detail outlined in the blueprint given to David by the Holy Spirit. "'Every part of this blueprint,' David told Solomon, 'was given to me in writing from the hand of the Lord.' Then he continued, 'Be strong and courageous and get to work. Don't be frightened by the size of the task, for the Lord my God is with you; he will not forsake you. He will see to it that everything is finished correctly'" (1 Chronicles 28:19–20 TLB).

Solomon not only had the blueprints or patterns to build the Temple of God. He also had the anointing and the authority to build it. Building the house of God would take more than just skilled laborers; Solomon would need to draw from his education founded upon wisdom, understanding, and knowledge. In building the house of God, He identified what is necessary to complete any assignment God gives to you—wisdom, understanding, and knowledge. "By wisdom a house is built, and by understanding it is established; by knowledge the rooms are filled with all precious and pleasant riches" (Proverbs 24:3–4 ESV).

THE INSTALLATION OF THE ARK

Generations of Israelites transported the Ark, the resting place of God's glory in the earth realm until King Solomon built the temple. God's creativity was released through blueprints and prototypes designated to establish worship. We see humanity having greater access to God's glory from generation to generation. The priest carried the Law or the Word of God given to Moses, stored in the Ark of the Covenant from the wilderness under Moses's leadership, then to Jerusalem under King David's supervision, and then to the Temple of Solomon. After the ark was placed in the temple, God's glory or presence manifested itself in the form of a cloud and filled the Temple of Solomon as it did in Moses's time.

Then the priests brought the ark of the covenant of the LORD to its place, into the inner sanctuary of the house, into the Holy of Holies, under the wings of the cherubim. There was nothing in the ark except the two tablets of stone which Moses put there at Horeb (Sinai), where the LORD made a covenant with the Israelites when they came out of the land of Egypt. Now it happened that when the priests had come out of the Holy Place, the cloud filled the LORD'S house, so the priests could not stand [in their positions] to minister because of the cloud, for the glory and brilliance of the LORD had filled the LORD'S house(temple). (1 Kings 8:6, 9–11 ESV)

In the article titled, "The Ark of the Covenant," the ark is called the Ark of Revelation. The priests were carrying a revelation of God's desire to commune with Israel and guide them continually. "Ark of the Covenant, Ark of the Revelation…are the full names of the sacred chest of acacia wood, overlaid with gold, which occupied the holiest place in the Tabernacle and temple, and through which the idea of the constant presence of the covenant of God with the people of Israel received symbolic expression. The Old Testament religion conceived of God as spiritual and so could not think to secure His presence by use of images."

Solomon prayed and dedicated the temple to the Lord. He understood the omnipresent nature of God; God could commune with Israel on earth, but God's dwelling place is heaven. When Solomon prayed, he revealed a pattern for entering the presence of God with praise and worship; he lifted his hands, praised God ("there is no God like you, in heaven above or on earth beneath"), and prayed the promise of God (A son of David would always be seated on the throne of Israel). Solomon also spoke of God's vastness and the existence of heavens that cannot contain the fullness of the presence of God (see 1 Kings 8:22–30).

SOLOMON'S SECOND VISITATION

After King Solomon prayed and dedicated the temple to the Lord, God appeared to Solomon a second time. The Lord reiterated the promise He made to David. One of his sons would always sit on the throne and rule the Kingdom of Israel. The promise illustrates David's legacy; the throne of David would exist eternally through Christ. "As soon as Solomon had finished building the house of the LORD and the king's house and all that Solomon desired to build, the LORD appeared to Solomon a second time, as he had appeared to him at Gibeon. And the LORD said to him, "'I have heard your prayer and your plea, which you have made before me. I have consecrated this house that you have built, by putting my name there forever. My eyes and my heart will be there for all time'" (1 Kings 9:1–3 ESV).

Visitations and dreams are a part of Solomon's spiritual inheritance. Dreamers tend to give birth to multiple generations of children who also are dreamers. There are four generations of dreamers of dreams in my family. Solomon's father was open to God's divine counsel and instructions even at night. The Scriptures below suggest that some of David's night encounters with God may have been dream encounters. He may have received much of his intimate understanding of the Lord and His coming kingdom through dreams.

> Let my vindication come from you; may your eyes see what is right. Though you probe my heart, though you examine me at night and test me, you will find that I have planned no evil; my mouth has not transgressed. (Psalm 17:2–3 NIV)

> I will bless the Lord who counsels me; he gives me wisdom in the night. He tells me what to do. (Psalm 16:7 TLB)

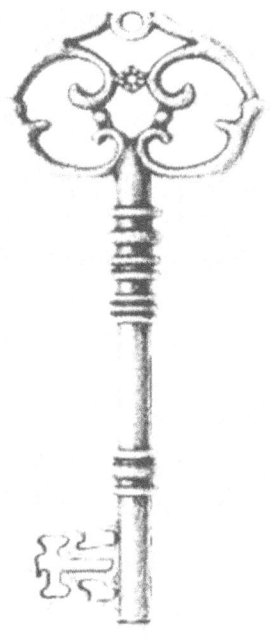

CHAPTER 4
CLOTHED IN HUMILITY

Before Solomon asked God for wisdom; he made a very significant statement. In 1 Kings 3:7 NLT, he says, "'Now, O LORD my God, you have made me king instead of my father, David, but I am like a little child who does not know his way around.'" Have you ever thought about how Solomon's description of himself as being "like a little child" who needs guidance would be so pleasing to the Lord? King Solomon illustrated humility; he likened himself to a child who needed to learn how to govern the people of God. What does it mean to be like a little child? Being like a little child means we must learn to trust the Lord like a child trusts his parents to meet his basic needs for food, shelter, and security. He learns to trust his parents through the care that he receives from his parents.

KEYS OF THE KINGDOM: REPENTANCE AND HUMILITY

When the disciples asked Jesus, who was the greatest in the kingdom, He told them unless they repented, and became like little children; they would not enter the kingdom of heaven. He revealed to the disciples that *humility* and *repentance* are keys to gaining access to the kingdom of heaven. According to *Vine's Complete Expository Dictionary of Old and New Testament Words*, the word repent infers 1. change your mind, the seat of moral reflection 2. regret 3. repentance from sin. Look at the Amplified version of the passage below and how it defines repent: "change your inner self—your old way of thinking, live changed lives."

> At that time the disciples came to Jesus and asked, "Who is greatest in the kingdom of heaven?" He called a little child and set him before them, and said, "I assure you *and* most solemnly say to you, unless you repent [that is, change your inner self—your old way of thinking, live changed lives] and become like children [trusting, humble, and forgiving], you will never enter the kingdom of heaven. Therefore, whoever humbles himself like this child is greatest in the kingdom of heaven." (Matthew 18:1–4 AMP)

In an interview on Family Life Blended Radio, Ron Deal said, "I've often wondered why there are lots of people who sit in church every week but only a few who put into practice what they learn. Proverbs 11 says, 'Pride leads to disgrace, but with humility comes wisdom.' The posture of humility acknowledges our dependence on God and opens us to the sanctifying work of the Holy Spirit. Pride closes you off to how the Lord wants to transform you. So, prepare your heart to receive God's wisdom." The specific Scripture referenced is Proverbs 11:2 NLT.

A dear friend was praying for me, and she said, "When you lay at the Father's feet, you are like a little girl." Laying at the Heavenly Father's feet is more than a phrase; it paints a picture of worship—an expression of love for the Father. It also paints a picture of humbling oneself when you lay down prostrate or kneel in the presence of God. Trust is necessary to grow in understanding of who God is and who we are in His kingdom. If we love, obey and trust God, we are His beloved sons and daughters.

Solomon referring to himself as being like a little child when it came to ruling the kingdom also shows how receptive he was to receive instructions and directions from God. His humility and trust in God opened the treasure troves of God. Solomon was able to receive divine revelation because of his understanding of humility. God places those in authority who are humble and receptive to the guidance of the Holy Spirit. The Word of God should govern leaders who have been given spiritual authority.

Therefore, I strongly urge the elders among you [pastors, spiritual leaders of the church, [called to testify] of the sufferings of Christ, as well as one who shares in the glory revealed: shepherd *and* guide *and* protect the flock of God among you, exercising oversight not under compulsion, but voluntarily, according to *the will of* God; and not [motivated] for shameful gain, but with wholehearted enthusiasm; not lording it over those assigned to your care [do not be arrogant or overbearing], but be examples [of Christian living] to the flock [set a pattern of integrity for your congregation]. (1 Peter 5:1–3 AMP)

Governing guidelines for pastors and leaders:

- Shepherd, guide, and protect
- Exercise oversight not under compulsion
- Do not be motivated by shameful gain
- Do not lord over those assigned to your care
- Be an example of Christian living
- Set a pattern of integrity

God gives us the grace to walk in a place of humility. He prepares our hearts to receive instruction from those he has placed in a position of authority. Scriptures poetically tell us to clothe ourselves in humility. *The KJV Dictionary* defines clothe as "to invest; to give to by commission; as, to *clothe* with power or authority." Clothing ourselves in humility empowers us for service in the kingdom of God.

Likewise, you younger men [of lesser rank and experience], be subject to your elders [seek their counsel]; and all of you, clothe yourselves with humility toward one another [tie on the servant's apron], for GOD IS OPPOSED TO THE PROUD [the disdainful, the presumptuous, and He defeats them], BUT HE GIVES GRACE TO THE HUMBLE. Therefore humble yourselves under the mighty hand of God [set aside self-righteous pride], so that He may exalt you [to a place of honor in His service] at the appropriate time. (1 Peter 5: 5–6 AMP)

Governing guidelines for a novice:

- Seek the counsel of an elder
- Clothe yourself with humility
- Humble yourself under the mighty hand of God

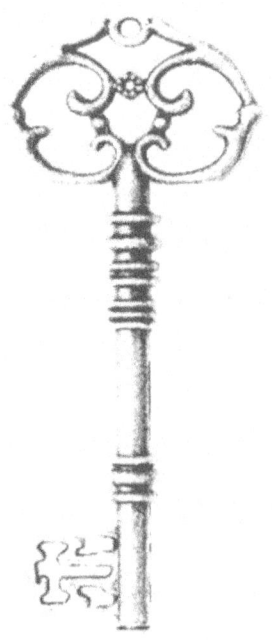

CHAPTER 5
THE MYSTERY OF WISDOM

Solomon's encounter with the Lord unlocked the mystery of wisdom. The Lord instructed Solomon on how to receive wisdom by first asking Solomon a question: "What do you want? Ask, and I will give it to you!" (1 Kings 3:5 NLT). Multiple Scriptures teach us to ask so that God can fulfill our needs. "If any of you lack wisdom, let him *ask of God*, that giveth to all men liberally, upbraideth not; and it shall be given him. But let him ask in faith, nothing wavering…" (James1:5–6, emphasis added). You can ask God to fill you with His Spirit if you have received salvation. Wisdom, understanding, and revelatory knowledge can be imparted when you ask God to fill you with His Holy Spirit. "For everyone who asks, receives. Everyone who seeks, finds. And to everyone who knocks, the door will be opened. 'You fathers—if your children ask for a fish, do you give them a snake instead? Or if they ask for an egg, do you give them a scorpion? Of course not! So if you sinful people know how to give good gifts to your children, how much more will your heavenly Father give the Holy Spirit to those who ask him'" (Luke 11:10–13 NLT).

Prayer to receive Holy Spirit:

God, I ask you to fill me with your Holy Spirit. Amen.

THE ORIGIN OF WISDOM

God made His mysteries known unto Solomon. He was given insight of the origin of wisdom. Solomon wrote about wisdom as an eyewitness giving an account of how God created the earth, heavens, and oceans. "The Lord formed me in the beginning, before he created anything else. From ages past, I am. I existed before the earth began. 'I was there when he established the heavens and formed the great springs in the depths of the oceans. I was there when he set the limits of the seas and gave them his instructions not to spread beyond their boundaries. I was there when he made the blueprint for the earth and oceans'" (Proverbs 8:22–23, 27–29 TLB).

What had been in the mind of God was translated into physical and spatial dimensions to illustrate God's creative power. It was revealed to Solomon that God used wisdom, understanding, and knowledge to create the earth, universe, and oceans. In Proverbs 3:19–20 TLB (emphasis added), Solomon wrote the following:

1. By *wisdom*, the Lord founded the earth.
2. By *understanding*, He created the universe and space (the heavens).
3. By His *knowledge*, the deep fountains broke open of the earth, and the skies poured down rain.

WISDOM UNLOCKS CREATIVITY

The wisdom that God revealed to Solomon in his dream unlocked different realms of creativity. He became a wordsmith, a skillful writer. He used words that could paint pictures in the minds of people who were hungry for personal application of God's wisdom in their lives. "He composed some 3,000 proverbs and wrote 1,005 songs. He could speak with authority about all kinds of plants, from the great cedar of Lebanon to the tiny hyssop that grows from cracks in a wall. He could also speak about animals, birds, small creatures, and fish" (1 Kings 4:32–33 NLT).

The KJV Dictionary defines a proverb as "a short sentence often repeated, expressing a well-known truth or common fact, ascertained by experience or observation; a maxim of wisdom." Solomon's amazing insight of wisdom allowed him to expound on its different dimensions and functions. When we hear wisdom, it can give divine instructions to unlock knowledge that releases creativity and understanding. Scriptures reveal that wisdom can also help unlock "knowledge of witty inventions." In Proverbs 8:8–12, wisdom speaks. "All the words of my mouth are in righteousness; there is nothing froward or perverse in them. They are all plain to him that understandeth, and right to them that find knowledge. Receive my instruction, and not silver; and knowledge rather than choice gold. For wisdom is better than rubies; and all the things that may be desired are not to be compared to it. In wisdom dwell with prudence, and find out knowledge of witty inventions." *Merriam Webster's Dictionary* defines witty as "having good intellectual capacity: intelligent."

The definition of invention points out that inventing is creating something that did not exist. It emphasizes the distinct difference between inventing something and discovering something, which gives us a greater insight into what it means to create something. God can give us a pattern or a blueprint for something that exists in heaven but not on earth, revealing yet another dimension of Himself, the Creator. *The KJV Dictionary* defines an invention as follows: "The action or operation of finding out something new; the contrivance of that which did not before exist; as the invention of logarithms; the invention of the art of printing; the invention of the orrery. Invention differs from discovery. Invention is applied to the contrivance and production of something that did not exist before. Discovery brings to light that which existed before, but which was not known."

THE PARADIGM OF EDUCATION

Proverbs are parables designed to develop wisdom, understanding, and knowledge that unlock mysteries. Throughout Proverbs, Solomon revealed a paradigm or a pattern for education rooted in the triad of wisdom, understanding, and knowledge. Proverbs 1:1-6 (AMP) outlines the purpose of proverbs; they develop the following:

1. Wisdom
2. Wise and moral behavior
3. Integrity
4. Critical thinking
5. Insight
6. Discernment
7. Ability to receive guidance and instructions
8. Knowledge and discretion
9. Capacity to learn
10. Receive and impart wise counsel
11. Understanding of proverbs (enigmas) and their interpretations
12. Understanding of parables and riddles

The wisdom, understanding, and knowledge God promised Solomon in his dream are evident in multiple Scriptures. The expansion of Solomon's spiritual and mental capacity enabled him to receive profound revelations. He wrote, "The fear of the Lord is the beginning of *wisdom*, and the *knowledge* of the Holy One is *understanding*" (Proverbs 9:10 NIV, emphasis added).

CREATIVITY AND DREAMS

In the Song of Solomon, one of Solomon's creative writings is written about a woman having a dream! In the dream, she states, " 'I was asleep, but my heart was awake...'" (Song of Solomon 5:2 AMP). In this dream sequence, Solomon wrote about the heart as the soul—the mind, will, emotions, and intellect. Song of Solomon 5 suggests that while we are physically asleep, we are spiritually awake, can interact in the dream realm with the Spirit of God, and discern our environment in the spiritual realm. As dreamers, we can receive insight concerning the spirit, soul, and body. The *Vine's Complete Expository Dictionary of Old and New Testament Words* states, "The heart, in its moral significance in the OT (Old Testament), includes the emotions, the reason and the will." It defines the heart as the following:

1. The seat of desire, inclination, or will be indicated by "heart": Pharaoh's heart is hardened" (Exod. 17:14).
2. The "heart" could be regarded as the seat of knowledge and wisdom and as a synonym for the "mind..." Solomon prayed, "Give therefore thy servant an understanding heart to judge thy people, that I may discern between good and bad" (1 Kings 3:9; cf. 4:29).
3. Memory is the activity of the "heart" as in Job 22:22 "... Lay up his [God's] words in thine heart."
4. The "heart" may be the seat of conscience and moral character. How does one respond to the revelation and the world around him? Job answers: "...my heart shall not reproach me as long as I live" (Job 27:6).

5. The "heart" is regarded as the seat of emotions: "And thou should love the Lord thy God with all thine heart..." (Deuteronomy 6:5).

In the dream, the woman is aware of her emotions and desires to be intimate with the one pursuing *her*, presumably, he is the Lord. However, she initially chooses to continue with her nightly ritual of preparing herself to sleep instead of opening the door to her "beloved." The woman's reluctance to open the door is much like reality when the Lord knocks at the door of your heart; you may be reluctant to allow him to come into all of the areas of your heart and life. The following passage beautifully illustrates how the Lord desires to have communion with us even as we sleep so that we can understand his heart and mind. "'I was asleep, but my heart was awake. A voice [in my dream]! My beloved was knocking: 'Open to me, my sister, my darling, My dove, my perfect one! For my head is drenched with the [heavy night] dew; My hair [is covered] with the dampness of the night.' 'I had taken off my dress, How can I put it on *again*? I had washed my feet, How could I get them dirty *again*?'" (Song of Solomon 5:2–3 AMP).

Once, the Lord said to me, "I long for you to long to be in my presence." The Lord wanted me to know that he wants to be pursued by me, like how the woman in the Song of Solomon later became love-sick for the Lord despite being beaten and wounded in her quest to find Him. Sometimes seeking this kind of intimacy with the Lord can be painful because people may misunderstand your passion for Him; they may not have experienced this kind of intimacy before in their relationship with

Him. When the woman felt compelled to open the door, her hands began to drip with oil; the oil represents the anointing. Seeking and longing to be in the presence of the Lord releases the anointing that He has placed in our lives—this is worship.

> "My beloved extended his hand through the opening [of the door], And my feelings were aroused for him. "I arose to open for my beloved; And my hands dripped with myrrh, And my fingers with liquid [sweet-scented] myrrh, On the handles of the bolt. "I opened for my beloved, But my beloved had turned away and was gone. My heart went out *to him* when he spoke. I searched for him, but I could not find him; I called him, but he did not answer me. "The watchmen who make the rounds in the city found me. They struck me, they wounded me; The guardsmen of the walls took my shawl from me. I command that you take an oath, O daughters of Jerusalem, If you find my beloved, As to what you tell him—[Say that] I am sick from love [sick from being without him]." (Song of Solomon 5:4–8 AMP)

Prophetic words can elevate your understanding of revelatory knowledge released in dreams. A young lady prophesied that I was "a spiritual archeologist." I have learned how to unlock biblical truths hidden in the Word of God, like how an archaeologist excavates treasures buried deep in the ground by multiple layers of dirt—one layer at a time to maintain the integrity of the articles being unearthed. The prophecy inspired me to remember this following dream about seeking wisdom.

THE DREAM

I was traveling by car along a road with my mother. We saw two young women in their twenties standing beside the road. It was raining, and I did not want to stop, but my mother told me to stop. I stopped, got out of the car, and began to dig in the ground. I found different sizes of foreign silver coins.

ANALYSIS AND INTERPRETATION OF THE DREAM

The most important elements in my dream are my mother, the two young women, the road, the car, the foreign silver coins, and the rain. My mother represents wisdom or a wise counselor. The college-age women represent a generation of believers in need of mentoring. The road represents the path that God had chosen for my life. The car represents a traveling ministry. The coins were foreign silver coins; they represent wisdom and revelation needed to minister to young people of different cultures and those who live in different countries. Digging in the ground represents seeking for wisdom and uncovering hidden things (mysteries). The rain represents divine inspiration—heavenly wisdom, understanding, and knowledge that I will need to fulfill my assignment, mentoring college-age young people internationally. The dream reflects when I am traveling along the path God has chosen for my life; I will have to discern if I am being led by God's Spirit or my personal desires.

If I did not stop, I might have missed an opportunity to receive the wisdom and revelation reserved along the path the Lord had predestined for my life.

You may be wondering how I knew the coins existed or where to dig for them. The Holy Spirit can direct you in your dreams the same way he leads you when you are awake. You will confidently know what you are supposed to do through the Spirit of God's guidance.

Holy Spirit uses our knowledge base, especially of Scriptures, to teach us. Meditation and memorization of Scriptures help us to build our knowledge base. I have read all the Scriptures in Proverbs multiple times and have memorized some of them. So, when I had this dream about seeking wisdom, I immediately knew it was an illustration of the following passage, which emphasizes that when we obey God's instruction, we can receive the wisdom and knowledge of God.

> Yes, if you cry out for insight, And lift up your voice for understanding; If you seek skillful *and* godly wisdom as you would silver And search for her as you would hidden treasures; Then you will understand the [reverent] fear of the LORD [that is, worshiping Him and regarding Him as truly awesome] And discover the knowledge of God. For the LORD gives [skillful and godly] wisdom; From His mouth come *knowledge* and *understanding*. He stores away sound *wisdom* for the righteous [those who are in right standing with Him]…(Proverbs 2:3–7 AMP, emphasis added)

The dream is also an illustration of the importance of having both wisdom and revelation. The Apostle Paul prayed for the church in Ephesus that God would give them a spirit of wisdom and revelation. He prayed that the eyes of their understanding (hearts and minds) would be flooded with light so they would have intimate knowledge of God and know His will for their lives.

> Therefore I also, after I heard of your faith in the Lord Jesus and your love for all the saints, do not cease to give thanks for you, making mention of you in my prayers: that the God of our Lord Jesus Christ, the Father of glory, may give to you the spirit of *wisdom* and *revelation* in the knowledge of Him, the eyes of your understanding being enlightened; that you may know what is the hope of His calling, what are the riches of the glory of His inheritance in the saints (Ephesians 1:15–18 NKJV, emphasis added).

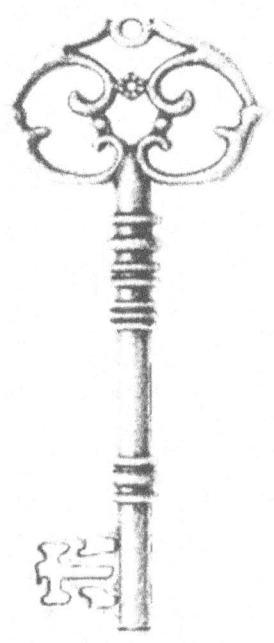

CHAPTER 6
A TYPE OF THE KING AND HIS KINGDOM

King Solomon asked God for a blueprint for ruling an earthly kingdom. He desired to see the will of God established and to rule with justice. Solomon is a type and shadow of Jesus who eternally rules God's kingdom with justice. Types and shadows help us to understand the plan and purpose that God has for man. "A type (from the Greek word *typos*) is a person, event, or institution in that signifies an even greater reality. The greater reality to which a type points and in which it finds its fulfillment is referred to as an *antitype*." The parallels between Jesus and Solomon are centered around their kingships and the throne of David, which was a part of the ancient Kingdom of Israel. They both received authority and the anointing to reign as kings. We must discuss David's throne to understand the extent of Solomon's and Jesus's kingdom. God sent the prophet Nathan to prophesy to David about his legacy. The prophecy is about Solomon building a temple for the presence of God. God promised to be with Solomon and establish David's throne forever. "'He shall build a house for my name, and I will establish the throne of his kingdom forever. And your house and your kingdom shall be made sure forever before me. Your throne shall be established forever'" (2 Samuel 7:13, 16 ESV).

This declaration about David's throne points us to Christ's eternal kingship as the King of Israel in heaven and earth as a son of David. The throne does not just represent a physical seat of power, but God's authority that would rest on all of David's sons appointed as king from Solomon to Christ throughout eternity. David is also a type and a shadow of Jesus as the King of Israel.

The parallels between Solomon and Jesus can also be understood when reading the prophecies concerning their births and lineage. The Prophet Isaiah saw many years into the future and eternity. He foretold the birth of Jesus and the authority He would have over the kingdom of God. His prophecy reveals to us that the throne that Jesus will sit on throughout eternity is the throne of David. Isaiah saw seven dimensions of Jesus's identity. "For to us a child is born, to us a son is given; and the government shall be upon his shoulder, and his name shall be called Wonderful Counselor, God, Everlasting Father, Prince of Peace. Of the increase of his government and of peace there will be no end, on the throne of David and over his kingdom to establish it and to uphold it with justice and with righteousness from this time forth and forevermore. The zeal of the LORD of hosts will do this" (Isaiah 9:6–7 ESV).

Seven different dimensions of Jesus's identity are as follow:

1. A child, the incarnate Living Word of God
2. The Son of God
3. A king
4. Wonderful Counselor
5. God
6. Everlasting Father
7. Prince of Peace

Isaiah prophesied about King David's lineage. His descendants would be a line of kings. Isaiah also prophesied about Jesus and His genealogy that stems from King David's father, Jesse. He prophesied that a rod would spring forth out of Jesse's stem, and a branch would grow out of his roots. According to *Vine's Complete Expository Dictionary of Old and New Testament Words*: 1.) rod refers to "a staff, a scepter." 2.) root refers to "cause, origin, source, said of persons and ancestors." The rod signifies that Jesus would be the King of Israel. A branch out of the root of Jesse signifies that Jesus is a descendant of David. "And there shall come forth a rod out of the stem of Jesse, and a Branch shall grow out of his roots: And the spirit of the LORD shall rest upon him, the spirit of wisdom and understanding, the spirit of counsel and might, the spirit of knowledge and of the fear of the LORD; And shall make him of quick understanding in the fear of the LORD..." (Isaiah 11:1–3).

Revelation 22:16 confirms that Jesus is a son of David. The Scripture also reveals two more dimensions of Jesus's identity; He is "the Root" and "bright Morning Star." Note that the verse below says first that Jesus is "the Root" and not a root. Secondly, it states that Jesus is David's Offspring and the "bright Morning Star." Being "the Root (the Source, the Life)" signifies that Jesus existed as the Word of God before anyone or anything existed. The name "bright Morning Star" signifies that Jesus is the Light of the World. "'I, Jesus, have sent My angel to testify to you *and* to give you assurance of these things for the churches. I am the Root (the Source, the Life) and the Offspring of David, the radiant *and* bright Morning Star'" (Revelation 22:16 AMP).

Solomon is a type of Jesus as the Prince of Peace. God promised David that Solomon would have peace throughout his life, unlike David, who fought many battles and wars. God promised to give Solomon rest from his enemies or peace. "Behold, a son shall be born to thee, who shall be a man of rest; and I will give him rest from all his enemies round about: for his name shall be Solomon, and I will give peace and quietness unto Israel in his days" (1 Chronicles 22:9).

Solomon and Jesus were known for possessing great wisdom, the wisdom of God. The wisdom that God had placed in Solomon's heart was immeasurable. Kings' ambassadors were sent from different parts of the world to receive divine counsel from him. "God gave Solomon very great wisdom and understanding, and knowledge as vast as the sands of the seashore. Solomon's wisdom was greater than the wisdom of all the people of the East, and greater than all the wisdom of Egypt. He was wiser than anyone else...And his fame spread to all the surrounding nations. From all nations people came to listen to Solomon's wisdom, sent by all the kings of the world, who had heard of his wisdom (1 Kings 4:29–31, 34 NLT).

Jesus was filled with wisdom and had the grace of God operating in His life even as a child. He had a profound dialogue with religious experts in a temple. Those who witnessed His interaction with these religious leaders were amazed at the wisdom that Jesus had as a young child. He increased in wisdom and the favor of God as He grew (see Luke 2:40–47).

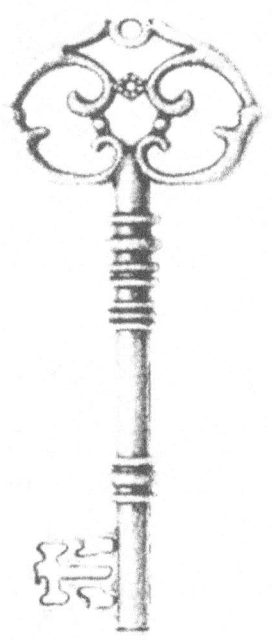

CHAPTER 7
GUARD YOUR HEART

According to Jack Hayford, in his book titled, *Majesty: God Enthroned in Our Worship*, "Worship means you are developing a set of values; you are establishing what holds first place in your life. Worship means you are determining what you are to become…The gods that one worships begin to manifest their attributes in the worshiper. Therefore, in deciding what or whom to worship, you are also making decisions about your values, priorities, and how you should live." In biblical times God warned the Israelites not to marry those who worshipped other gods because they would be able to corrupt their hearts. Though Solomon wrote in Proverbs 4:23 NLT, "Guard your heart above all else, for it determines the course of your life;" his heart became corrupted. Solomon disobeyed God, married 700 women from different nations, and had 300 concubines. Solomon built temples or shrines for all of his foreign wives' gods. He no longer was totally devoted to God; his desires had changed (see 1 Kings 11:1–4).

The KJV Dictionary defines idolatry as "The worship of idols, images, or anything made by hands, or which is not God. Idolatry is of two kinds; the worship of images, statues, pictures, made by hands; and the worship of the heavenly bodies, the sun, moon and stars, or of demons, angels, men and animals." Psalm 115 outlines the dangers of constructing idols and engaging in idolatry. Like in biblical times, if a person makes an idol out of another person or engages in ungodly worship, they risk losing their voice, insight, discernment, fellowship with God, prayer life, and spiritual identity. "The idols [of the nations] are silver and gold, The work of man's hands. They have mouths, but they cannot speak; They have eyes, but they cannot see; They have ears, but they cannot hear; They have noses, but they cannot smell; They have hands, but they cannot feel; They have feet, but they cannot walk; Nor can they make a sound with their throats. Those who make them will become like them, Everyone who trusts in them" (Psalm 115:4–8 AMP).

THE IMPORTANCE OF GUARDING YOUR HEART

The purpose of guarding your heart is to maintain the health of your soul (mind, will, emotions, and intellect) and relationship with the Lord. Guarding your heart helps align you with God's Word and His will. It also helps keep you sensitive to the guidance of the Holy Spirit.

I have seen spiritually wounded people continue to minister to others while they needed inner healing and deliverance. Like Solomon, their hearts had become corrupted; they started teaching another gospel—using the Word of God to justify beliefs, behaviors, and actions contrary to the Bible. One of the ways to guard your heart is by meditating on the Scriptures daily. Scriptural meditation can bring healing to the spirit, soul, and body. "'You will keep in perfect and constant peace the one whose mind is steadfast [that is, committed and focused on You—in both inclination and character], Because he trusts and takes refuge in You [with hope and confident expectation]'" (Isaiah 26:3 AMP).

PART II

DREAMS AND TRANSFORMATION OF THE MIND

CHAPTER 8
DREAMS AND REVELATORY KNOWLEDGE

Dreams can disclose information that brings freedom from abusive relationships, environments, and unhealthy systems. November 11, 2006, I had a dream about keys that could unlock my understanding and a path to my destiny. I was standing in an unfamiliar place with people whom I attended church. Our pastor was standing in front of us as though he was going to address us; he remained silent. While waiting for him to speak, I noticed that everyone was wearing what natives of India would wear: long-sleeved shirts and pants. I was lifted to a high place and looked down at the people. Though everyone else was calm, I became conscious of how I felt—afraid and anxious. I was suddenly standing at ground level again, and two skeleton keys appeared in my right hand, one silver, and the other gold. Then the dream shifted, and I was standing somewhere else outdoors with a friend and our pastor. My friend said to me, "Your team needs you." Our pastor angrily said, "If she wants to leave, let her." Then I said, "God, why are they so angry with me? —When all I did was get out of the box." That was the end of the dream.

After I woke up, my first thought was, *Oh my goodness, I have been in a box*. I immediately began to write down the dream. I did not understand some things about my dream until months later. I was unaware that I was in a box until I woke up and thought about my question. *God, why are they so angry with me? —When all I did was get out of the box*. I did not understand the reality of my situation until I woke up physically and then spiritually. I became aware that I was not only locked into an unhealthy state of mind and system; I was being contained.

ANALYSIS AND INTERPRETATION OF THE DREAM

Let's begin analyzing the individual parts or components of the dream to understand the dream's specific meaning. Then we will delve even deeper into the dream by investigating how the dream's parts relate to the dream as a whole. The careful analysis of this dream is crucial because it is about being set free from a system that can cause you to become bound in your mind and unable to discern the Spirit of God from the spirit of the world. Lack of discernment can leave us unable to determine what is true or false concerning Scriptures, reality, and God's original intent for our lives.

THE BOX

The box represents a frame of mind or a mindset and explicitly represents a closed mind. No one can escape this system without a revelation from the Lord. This box had a floor with walls and multi-level ceilings. The box's purpose was to keep us contained and stopped from reaching our potential. I also knew the box, not just the walls—was invisible. The walls of the box were control, manipulation, intimidation, and fear. I knew that the other people in the box did not know they were in a box because they were calm. I could not see what was going on outside of the box until I was outside of the box. When we are entangled in a situation, we may not understand how unhealthy it is until we are separated from the people and the conditions that have created the situation.

CEILINGS

The Holy Spirit revealed to me that this box had three different heights of ceilings (e.g., 12 feet, 15 feet, and 18 feet). The three different ceilings created an illusion of being elevated to higher levels of understanding without limitations. The multi-level ceilings were used to conceal the truth: I had been locked into a controlling system and frame of mind designed to inhibit spiritual growth and development. Once I had reached the highest ceiling in the box, I could sense something was wrong, but I still did not know that I was in a box. Being locked in the box, I could not go beyond the level of understanding I had been at far too long.

Sometimes ceilings or barriers are strongholds; strongholds can be unhealthy thought patterns and ideas that prevent us from breaking through to higher levels of understanding our spiritual identity. A revelation can help us break through barriers, unhealthy thought patterns, and systems designed to keep us from recognizing the authority given to us as citizens of the kingdom of heaven. *The Cambridge Dictionary* defines revelation as "the act of making something known that was a secret or a fact that has been made known."

THE CLOTHING

In my dream, people were dressed like our pastor in light blue clothing, which represents idolatry and conformity, not unity. Conformity is "the process whereby people change their beliefs, attitudes, action, or perceptions to more closely match those held by groups to which they belong or want to belong or by groups whose approval they desired." While we might admire a person because of their gifts and accomplishments, it is not always healthy to emulate a person. God wants sons and daughters, not clones. Sometimes controlling church leaders want to rid their members of all expressions of individuality. When the members give up their individuality to please the leader, it creates a false expression of unity and humility. The Scriptures encourage us to be imitators of God.

> Therefore become imitators of God [copy Him and follow His example], as well-beloved children [imitate their father]; and walk

continually in love [that is, value one another—practice empathy and compassion, unselfishly seeking the best for others], just as Christ also loved you and gave Himself up for us, an offering and sacrifice to God [slain for you, so that it became] a sweet fragrance. (Ephesians 5:1–2 AMP)

The Bible encourages us to be clothed with Christ. Being clothed with Christ is exhibiting the character of Christ. This is also how we become imitators of God instead of men. "For you [who are born-again have been reborn from above—spiritually transformed, renewed, sanctified and] are all children of God [set apart for His purpose with full rights and privileges] through faith in Christ Jesus. For all of you who were baptized into Christ [into a spiritual union with the Christ, the Anointed] have clothed yourselves with Christ [that is, you have taken on His characteristics and values]" (Galatians 3:26–27 AMP).

We can also be clothed with Christ and imitators of God by having the mind of Christ. Having the mind of Christ means having the same mentality that Jesus has. He came to represent God on the earth and to serve humanity. Jesus also came to teach us how we should live as citizens of the kingdom of God. People will be inspired to serve God because they see how we live.

THE SILENCE

What did waiting for our pastor to address us as we stood silently represent? The silence represents a loss of understanding that our individual voices are important. Having a voice signifies that we have value. When we listen to what others say, we let them know that what they have to say is important, even if we disagree. In environments or systems where there is a lot of control and intimidation, it is easy to lose understanding of the importance of our voices.

THE KEYS

In dreams, keys can unlock wisdom and revelation. Spiritual keys or spiritual authority are also designed to set one free from the captivity in the mind created by false teachings and spiritual abuse. Spiritual abuse can result from someone using Scriptures, their position, or authority in a ministry to control another person.

In my dream, keys—one silver and one gold—appeared in my right hand. Silver represents "the Word of God, wisdom, redemption, divinity, righteousness, strengthened faith by fire, and refining." Gold represents "eternal deity, the Godhead, glory, purification, majesty, righteousness, divine light, kingliness, trial by fire, and victory." The silver key was to unlock my mind or understanding so that I could take authority over strongholds—unhealthy thought patterns. The gold key was to unlock the glory of God (the presence of God) that releases transformation and revelation to teach the gospel of the kingdom.

I had reached my highest level of growth in an enclosed setting; then, I received the keys. I had to receive a revelation that I was being contained spiritually, mentally, and emotionally to escape the system within the box. These keys can unlock revelatory knowledge stored in the Scriptures to move us beyond the boundaries and limitations that keep us from being elevated in our understanding of the kingdom of God. Keys or authority come with a revelation and an assignment. The Lord does not just set us free; He gives us the power to become His witnesses to testify about the gospel of the kingdom of heaven. When the presence of God is released to deliver us, an anointing and authority can be released simultaneously to give us the power to do the same for others as a demonstration of the power of God.

The keys that were given to me not only represent authority but dominion. We can take authority over demonic systems and thoughts that try to infiltrate our minds. I needed to understand that my dream was about a system designed to captivate the mind. This system is designed to contain and suppress us from reaching a higher understanding of our spiritual capacity and identity. Systems built on man's beliefs and not the Bible exist in the spiritual realm. These systems can blind the mind to the gospel of the kingdom. They can also keep us from going beyond the four walls of the church to communities and nations. "See to it that no one takes you captive by philosophy and empty deceit, according to human tradition, according to the elemental spirits of the world, and not according to Christ" (Colossians 2:8 ESV).

The Apostle Paul also wrote about casting down vain imaginations and taking authority over them by bringing our thoughts into the obedience of Christ. Vain imaginations can also be a stronghold. Strongholds are referred to as fortresses in the following Scripture. "The weapons of our warfare are not physical [weapons of flesh and blood]. Our weapons are divinely powerful for the destruction of fortresses. We are destroying sophisticated arguments and every exalted and proud thing that sets itself up against the [true] knowledge of God, and we are taking every thought and purpose captive to the obedience of Christ" (2 Corinthians 10:4–5 AMP).

The Lord had set me free from an unhealthy mindset and system. The Lord is able to transcend physical and spiritual barriers, including those that may exist in the depths of our minds. When we receive a revelation, the light of the Lord can begin to shine into the dark corners of our minds and reveal our hearts' condition. When we repent from misguided loyalties and embracing false doctrines, the Lord can intervene by releasing an anointing that delivers us from systems built on idolatry and ignorance.

THE VEIL

Scriptures point out that a veil exists over our hearts until we decide to change and follow Christ. This veil represents a closed mind or spiritual blindness that creates an inability to understand the truth concealed in the Scriptures. *Vine's Complete Expository Dictionary of Old and New Testament Words* defines the veil as "metaphorically of the spiritually darkened vision suffered retributively by Israel until the conversion of the nation to their Messiah takes place." The Scriptures cite that Jesus is the only one who can remove the veil. When Jesus removes the veil, we can experience freedom, become more like Christ, and a reflection of God's glory, the light that comes from spending time in the presence of God. Some people have prayed to receive salvation but have not made Jesus

DREAMS AND REVELATORY KNOWLEDGE | 95

Lord over their lives. They have submitted themselves to the lordship of men, but until they decide to change and follow Christ, the veil of spiritual blindness will remain over their hearts and minds.

> We are not like Moses, who put a covering over his face. He covered his face so that the people of Israel would not see it. The glory was disappearing, and Moses did not want them to see it end. But their minds were closed. And even today, when those people read the writings of the old agreement, that same covering hides the meaning. That covering has not been removed for them. It is taken away only through Christ. Yes, even today, when they read the Law of Moses, there is a covering over their minds. But when someone changes and follows the Lord, that covering is taken away. The Lord is the Spirit, and where the Spirit of the Lord is, there is freedom. And our faces are not covered. We all show the Lord's glory, and we are being changed to be like him. This change in us brings more and more glory, which comes from the Lord, who is the Spirit. (2 Corinthians 3:13–18 ERV)

Our belief systems, values, and culture shape the way we think. Our church organizations and educational institutions also influence how we process ideas, concepts, and thoughts. The Lord kept gradually releasing revelation to me to interpret this dream as I received emotional healing. The more complex the dream is, the more time it may take to interpret it. I prayed and meditated on Scriptures relevant to the most significant elements in the dream.

DREAM INTERPRETATION AND PRAYER

Joseph and Daniel vocalized that God gives dreams and their interpretations. In the book of Daniel, we see that God is not only the giver of the interpretation of dreams but that he could also reveal the content of King Nebuchadnezzar's dream to Daniel when the king had forgotten the dream. Prayer was one source of Daniel's spiritual strength and ability to interpret dreams. "'Thus says the LORD who made *the earth*, the LORD who formed it to establish it—the LORD is His name,' Call to Me and I will answer you, and tell you [and even show you] great and mighty things, [things which have been confined and hidden], which you do not know *and* understand *and* cannot distinguish'" (Jeremiah 33:2–3 AMP).

In the Old Testament, "secret" can also mean a dream. When we do not remember a dream, the Holy Spirit may reveal the information at a later appointed time. The information in the king's dream was concealed so that God would be glorified through Daniel. God revealed the secret or the king's dream to Daniel in a "vision of the night," indicating Daniel's great weight of authority in both the spiritual and dream realm.

> Then Daniel went to his house, and made the decision known to Hananiah, Mishael, and Azariah, his companions, that they might seek mercies from the God of heaven concerning this secret…Then the secret was revealed to Daniel in a night vision. So Daniel blessed the God of heaven. Daniel answered and said: "Blessed be the name of God forever and ever, For *wisdom* and might are His. And He changes the times and the seasons; He

removes kings and raises up kings; He gives *wisdom* to the wise And *knowledge* to those who have *understanding*. He reveals deep and secret things; He knows what *is* in the darkness, And light dwells with Him." (Daniel 2:17–22 NKJV, emphasis added)

The king had a complex dream—a dream and visions within the dream. Daniel indirectly explained how the content of the king's dream and its interpretation were revealed to him by God's wisdom; he said that the secret was not revealed to him because he had more wisdom (intelligence) than anyone else. Daniel told the king that the "mightiest" or God knows the thoughts of his heart. He explained to King Nebuchadnezzar that God had given him revelatory knowledge concerning the future.

Daniel answered in the king's presence and said, "The secret which the king has demanded, the wise *men*, the astrologers, the magicians, and the soothsayers cannot declare to the king. But there is a God in heaven who reveals secrets, and He has made known to King Nebuchadnezzar what will be in the latter days. Your dream, and the visions of your head upon your bed, were these: As for you, O king, thoughts came *to* your *mind while* on your bed, *about* what would come to pass after this; and He who reveals secrets has made known to you what will be. But as for me, this secret has not been revealed to me because I have more wisdom than anyone living, but for *our* sakes who make known the interpretation to the king, and that you may know *the thoughts of your heart*." (Daniel 2:27–30 NKJV, emphasis added)

Look at the language in the latter Scriptures of the above passage that Daniel uses in reference to the king's visions within his dream. He referred to the king's visions as the "thoughts" of his heart. Remember that dreams can reveal what is in the mind and heart of God concerning a person, past, present, or future event. Daniel equated the king's visions to the thoughts of God, downloaded into the heart and mind of the king. The king would know what was in the mind and heart of God concerning the future.

THE KING'S DREAM

God had given the king a dream of a giant statue, a stone, and a mountain. Different segments of the statue were made of five different materials:

1. The head was made of gold.
2. The chest and arms were made of silver.
3. The belly and thighs were made of bronze.
4. The lower legs were made of iron.
5. The feet were made of a mixture of iron and baked clay.

The king watched the stone be cut but without hands. The stone crushed the feet of the statue; the statue was destroyed without a trace that it had ever existed. Then, the king saw the stone become a mountain that filled the earth

"You, O king, were looking, and behold, [there was] a single great statue;…As for this statue, its head *was made* of fine gold, its breast and its arms of silver, its belly and its thighs of bronze, its legs of iron, its feet partly of iron and partly of clay [pottery]. As you were looking, a stone was cut out without [human] hands, and it struck the statue on its feet of iron and clay and crushed them. Then the iron, the clay, the bronze, the silver, and the gold were crushed together and became like the chaff from the summer threshing floors; and the wind carried them away so that not a trace of them could be found. And the stone that struck the statue became a great mountain and filled the whole earth." (Daniel 2:31–35 NKJV)

THE UNLOCKING OF A KING'S IDENTITY AND DESTINY

God used the dream's interpretation to unlock King Nebuchadnezzar's identity and destiny. God had given King Nebuchadnezzar a kingdom and dominion throughout the earth. "You, O king, are a king of kings. For the God of heaven has given you a kingdom, power, strength, and glory; and wherever the children of men dwell, or the beasts of the field and the birds of the heaven, He has given them into your hand, and has made you ruler over them all—you are this head of gold" (Daniel 2:37–38 NKJV).

The dream symbolizes the rise and fall of ancient kingdoms (the five different segments of the statue). Daniel discussed the sequence of the rise and fall of kingdoms that would come after King Nebuchadnezzar's kingdom, the Babylonian Kingdom. These kingdoms would be replaced by the eternal kingdom of God (the mountain), whose eternal King is Jesus.

> But after you shall arise another kingdom inferior to yours; then another, a third kingdom of bronze, which shall rule over all the earth. And the fourth kingdom shall be as strong as iron, inasmuch as iron breaks in pieces and shatters everything; and like iron that crushes, *that kingdom* will break in pieces and crush all the others. And in the days of these kings the God of heaven will set up a kingdom which shall never be destroyed; and the kingdom shall not be left to other people; it shall break in pieces and consume all these kingdoms, and it shall stand forever. (Daniel 2:39–40, 44 NKJV)

The dream points to King Nebuchadnezzar as a type and a shadow of Jesus as King of kings and Lord of lords. The inscription on Jesus's robe and thigh in the book of Revelation confirms this. "And He has on *His* robe and on His thigh a name written: KING OF KINGS AND LORD OF LORDS" (Revelation 19:16 NKJV). God made King Nebuchadnezzar a world ruler. The dream also illustrates how God reveals Himself in dreams, and it inspired the king to give Daniel a promotion. "The king answered Daniel, and said, 'Truly your God *is* the God of gods, the Lord of kings, and a revealer of secrets, since you could reveal this secret.' Then the king promoted Daniel and gave him many great gifts; and he made him ruler over the whole province of Babylon, and chief administrator over all the wise *men* of Babylon" (Daniel 2:47–48 NKJV).

MANTLES AND MYSTERIES

Like Joseph, Daniel had a mantle—an anointing and authority to understand God's mysteries through dreams and visions. Two of the highest-ranking government officials of Joseph's and Daniel's time (The King of Egypt and King Nebuchadnezzar) were given divine counsel through dream interpretation. Joseph and Daniel had a divine connection to the Spirit of God and were guided by His wisdom. God reveals His secrets to His people, His sons and daughters—those who are led by His Spirit. " 'He uncovers mysteries [that are difficult to grasp and understand] out of the darkness...' " (Job 12:22 AMP).

DIFFERENT LEVELS OF DREAM INTERPRETATION

Pharaoh and King Nebuchadnezzar needed men who could understand the heart and mind of God to interpret their dreams. Joseph and Daniel were very connected to the Holy Spirit; those in authority within the foreign systems they lived in acknowledged that they had wisdom others did not have. Daniel and the friends that prayed with him had the wisdom of God. Their spiritual and intellectual capacity exceeded all others that the king consulted; their relationship with the Lord and education unlocked their understanding.

> God gave these four young men an unusual aptitude for understanding every aspect of literature and wisdom. And God gave Daniel the special ability to interpret the meanings of visions and dreams. When the training period ordered by the king was completed, the chief of staff brought all the young men

to King Nebuchadnezzar. The king talked with them, and no one impressed him as much as Daniel, Hananiah, Mishael, and Azariah. So they entered the royal service. Whenever the king consulted them in any matter requiring wisdom and balanced judgment, he found them ten times more capable than any of the magicians and enchanters in his entire kingdom. (Daniel 1:17–20 NLT)

When we have received the infilling of the Holy Spirit, we can operate in the gifts of the Holy Spirit and interpret dreams on a higher level. Praying in tongues and in the spirit to receive the interpretation is a higher form of dream interpretation than analyzing the symbols in dreams. However, all levels of dream interpretation require prayer. I have prayed in tongues about a dream, and the interpretation of tongues was the dream's interpretation. According to the study series, *The Holy Spirit and His Gifts*, the gifts of speaking in tongues and the interpretation of tongues are equivalent to prophesying. Dreams can have the same purpose as prophecy: to encourage, comfort, and equip. The following passage says that when we speak in tongues, we are speaking mysteries.

For one who speaks in an *unknown* tongue does not speak to people but to God; for no one understands him *or* catches his meaning, but by the Spirit he speaks mysteries [secret truths, hidden things]. But [on the other hand] the one who prophesies speaks to people for edification [to promote their spiritual growth] and speaks words of] encouragement [to uphold and advise them concerning the matters of God] and [speaks words of] consolation [to matters compassionately comfort them]. (1 Corinthians 14:2–3 AMP)

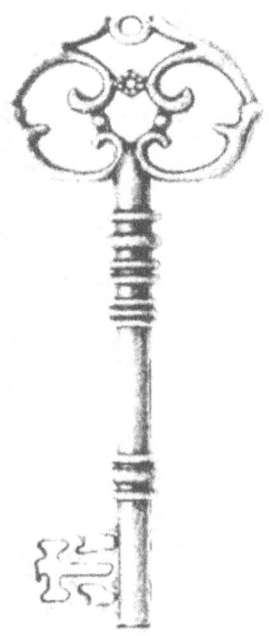

CHAPTER 9
SYSTEMS

Daniel and Joseph were promoted within the foreign systems or kingdoms they lived in because of God's wisdom manifested through their ability to interpret dreams. Systems designed to oppress them helped to cultivate their gifts. Dreaming of a system you are a part of can reveal intimate knowledge or inside information about it. You can learn the system's effect on a person's mind, perception, and spiritual growth. One of the best on-screen illustrations of a system with the power to enslave one's mind is *The Matrix*. The matrix was a complex system created by machines to create the illusion of a natural world in the person's mind, who was physically connected to the matrix through their central nervous system (brain and spinal cord). The main character, Neo experienced an awakening to the reality of a post-apocalyptic world after being disconnected from the matrix. The other main character, Morpheus, initially helped Neo disconnect from the system physically, then emotionally, and mentally. Morpheus explained the following to Neo: "The matrix is a system. That system is our enemy. When you are inside, you look around. What do you see? Lawyers, businessmen, teachers, carpenters. The very minds of the people that we are trying to save, but until we do, these people are still a part of this system, and that makes them our enemy. You have to understand that most of these people are not ready to be unplugged and many of them are so inert, hopelessly dependent on the system that they will fight to protect it."

When people are a part of a controlling system, they sometimes behave as though they have been conditioned or programmed how to think. After changing churches, I was confronted by people I attended church with when I had the dream about being in a box. One person asked me, "Did pastor release you?" Another person asked, "Does pastor know you are doing missions?" If you have been a part of a church with controlling leaders, then you know these questions are symptomatic of being programmed to believe we must often have the pastor's permission before making personal decisions.

I started attending another church with some of the leaders from my former church. I thought our dialogue and communication would change because we were under different pastoral leadership. However, our interactions with one another were the same; they expected me to continue to be overly submissive towards them instead of just showing respect. I began to question myself: *How did I get back inside the box?* I realized I had not left the box. I left the box when I stopped idolizing people in leadership and let go of their false expectations and responsibilities. Then I began to understand the importance of having boundaries. We must have boundaries to prevent ourselves from being locked into systems designed to hinder our spiritual growth. Look at the following Scriptures that can help us to establish healthy boundaries.

1. We must learn to say no when what is being asked of us goes against the will and Word of God. The disciples were threatened not to teach in the name of Jesus, and they refused to conform.

The apostles were brought in and made to appear before the Sanhedrin to be questioned by the high priest. "We gave you strict orders not to teach in this name," he said. "Yet you have filled Jerusalem with your teaching and are determined to make us guilty of this man's blood.'" Peter and the other apostles replied: "We must obey God rather than human beings!" (Acts 5:27–29 NIV)

2. When we choose to worship God, we are forbidden to worship another god.

The devil led him up to a high place and showed him in an instant all the kingdoms of the world And he said to him, "I will give you all their authority and splendor; it has been given to me, and I can give it to anyone I want to. If you worship me, it will all be yours." Jesus answered, "It is written: 'Worship the Lord your God and serve him only.'" (Luke 4:5–8 NIV)

3. We are to live by the Word of God and not by our desires.

After fasting forty days and forty nights, he was hungry. The tempter came to him and said, "If you are the Son of God, tell these stones to become bread." Jesus answered, "It is written: 'Man shall not live on bread alone, but on every word that comes from the mouth of God.'" (Matthew 4:2–4 NIV)

Systems are illustrated in both the Old and the New Testaments of the Bible. They are important because they give us structure and order to function in our daily lives. However, the illustration in my dream of being in a box was an unhealthy system within a church organization, but it is not limited to church organizations. Though I had learned so much from my former church, the environment shaping my spiritual life had become very unhealthy for me. I was receiving scriptural teaching, but I desired a greater depth of knowledge and understanding of the Word of God. I felt like I had come to a standstill in my spiritual growth. I had been growing by leaps and bounds since I had begun to attend this church. I did not know that what I had been experiencing was an illusion until the Holy Spirit began to give me the interpretation of the dream. I equated spiritual growth with spiritual health; though I loved serving in this ministry, I had become very exhausted and dissatisfied with where I was spiritually. The Lord told me that when I feel dissatisfied, it means go to another level. I needed to change some of my relationships and my mindset. I had been locked into a mindset and suppressed by a system. I never thought the revelation I needed to be liberated from the prison in my mind created by manipulation, control, intimidation, and fear would come from dreams.

Serving in church is very important. However, God does not want us to become slaves to a system of service. Supporting someone else's ministry does not require us to neglect the ministries he has given us. I had grown spiritually serving in my church but did not understand how to function in my purpose until I started traveling and participating in mission trips. You have probably heard the saying by Thomas Jefferson, "If you want something that you have never had before, then you must do something that you have never done before." I had never traveled outside the United States until I participated in my first mission trip to Cambodia and China. It was an amazing experience; I received exposure to the beauty of cultures very different from mine. I would never think about life the way I used to when I returned home. Oliver Wendell Holmes said, "Man's mind, once stretched by a new idea, never regains its original dimensions." My mind and worldview had expanded.

THE WORLD'S PATTERN AND CONFORMITY

Revelatory knowledge is needed to keep a person from going back into the box or an unhealthy frame of mind. Unless we renew our minds, we can go from church to church and never be free from oppressive systems and strongholds. What we believe affects how we think, act, and communicate. "May the words of my mouth and the meditation of my heart be pleasing to you, O LORD, my rock and my redeemer" (Psalm 19:14 NLT).

I had treated the box as though it existed only in one environment or place. I discovered that the box existed in the spiritual realm. It also represented the dysfunction in my mind keeping me from breakthroughs. However, dreaming about the box helped me to identify my spiritual condition and change how I thought. Look at three different translations of the following Scripture, Romans 12:2.

> Do not conform to the pattern of this world, but be transformed by the renewing of your mind. Then you will be able to test and approve what God's will is—his good, pleasing and perfect will. (NIV)

> Do not copy the behavior and customs of this world, but let God transform you into a new person by changing the way you think. Then you will learn to know God's will for you, which is good and pleasing and perfect. (NLT)

Do not be conformed to this world, but be transformed by the renewal of your mind, that by testing you may discern what is the will of God, what is good acceptable and perfect. (ESV)

Look at the emphasis in each Scripture:

- Do not follow the patterns of this world.
- Do not copy the traditions—the behavior and customs of the world.
- Do not be conformed to this world.
- Be transformed.

Do you see what all of these different translations of Romans 12:2 have in common? We should not conform to the world's systems' ways, patterns, customs, or traditions. We should be transformed in our minds daily by reading and meditating on the Scriptures so we may know the will of God for our lives. Our thoughts are important; they influence how we communicate and relate to others.

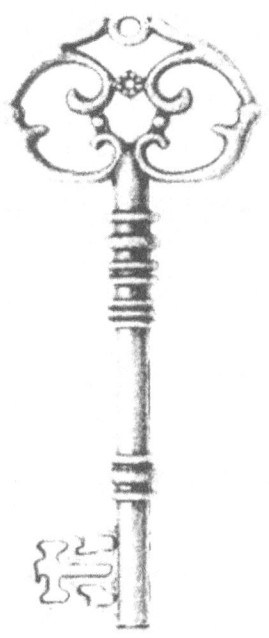

CHAPTER 10
TECHNOLOGY AND SPIRITUAL CAPACITY

Years ago, the Prayer of Jabez became popular after a book called *The Prayer of Jabez: Breakthrough to the Blessed Life* was published. I began to pray to enlarge my territory, an excerpt from the prayer of Jabez. "And Jabez called on the God of Israel saying, 'Oh, that You would bless me indeed, and enlarge my territory, that Your hand would be with me, and that You would keep *me* from evil, that I may not cause pain!' So God granted him what he requested" (1 Chronicles 4:10 NKJV). Years later, the Lord said to me, "Pray, increase my spiritual capacity." In a message, *How to Engage the Anointing to Be an Overcomer*, Dr. Cindy Trimm, a phenomenal Bible teacher, stated, "The Jabez anointing is an enlargement of territory, but the territory that the Jabez anointing actually releases is intellectual property, intellectual territories. It expands it. It actually upgrades it so that you are able to receive what the natural mind cannot receive. You're able to have the capacity to carry an anointing that taps in. It gives you a direct line to heaven, a direct line to the mind of God so that your prayers don't have to be verbose…" Her insight is significant because it emphasizes expanding the intellect, instead of physical land, to increase our effectiveness in prayer and problem solving with understanding beyond our natural means.

THE DREAM

Five years ago I had a dream about computer chips. I was eating breakfast in a restaurant. When the waitress brought me the bill, it looked like she had brought the whole register receipt roll. I thought, *I know I ate a lot, but I don't think I ate that much.* I looked down at my plate, which had six small black computer chips on it, and I ate three of them. When the waitress returned to close out my bill, I told her that I had eaten three of the computer chips and that they were quite tasty and tasted like bacon. Then I woke up.

ANALYSIS AND INTERPRETATION OF THE DREAM

The Lord told me to think about what a computer can do when you upgrade it or add more memory (RAM, Random Access Memory). According to the article, "What Is Random Access Memory (RAM)?"

adding or upgrading this type of memory improves the computer system's performance and allows the computer to work with more information simultaneously. I believe the Holy Spirit can teach us how to process information that He downloads to us, much like the computer does, all at the same time, giving us the ability to receive revelation more quickly.

Microchips mimic the brain's ability to store information as memory. A computer has a capacity or a limit on how much memory you can add. The more memory you add, the faster programs on your computer can work. Unlike the computer, I believe our minds have an immeasurable capacity to be upgraded.

God had given me an upgrade and increased my spiritual capacity. I could receive revelation more quickly and recall more information speedily. As we grow spiritually, so does our capacity to receive revelation. I had eaten only three of the six microchips on the plate in the dream, so I have memory with information, specifically revelatory knowledge being reserved for an appointed time.

A receipt is a record of what we have purchased; however, it was a record of what I had eaten or consumed spiritually. God had fed or downloaded a large amount of information into my spirit. Eating in a dream can represent receiving revelatory knowledge to complete an assignment. Before Ezekiel was sent to prophesy to the house of Israel, the Lord gave him a scroll to eat. A prophecy was downloaded into Ezekiel's spirit by ingesting the Word of God in the form of a scroll. "He said to me, 'Son of man, eat what you find [in this book]; eat this scroll, then go, speak to the house of Israel.' So I opened my mouth, and He fed me the scroll. He said to me, 'Son of man, eat this scroll that I am giving you and fill your stomach with it.' So I ate it, and it was as sweet as honey in my mouth. Then He said to me, 'Son of man, go to the house of Israel and speak My words to them'" (Ezekiel 3:1–4 AMP).

Dreaming of innovative technology is symbolic of receiving revelatory knowledge. It illustrates increasing one's spiritual capacity by downloading information into your spirit that transforms your mind. Dreaming of technology also signifies a paradigm shift, "a significant change that happens when a new and different way replaces the usual way of thinking about or doing something."

A simple definition of paradigm is an example or pattern. We experienced a paradigm shift when we changed from analog to digital technology. If you wanted to continue to watch television, you had to buy a converter box or have a cable television subscription.

A retired math teacher prophesied to me while on a mission trip. The math teacher, a young man, and I were praying on the third floor of a cruise ship. The math teacher touched me on the side of my head and said, "He (meaning the Holy Spirit) is expanding your mind exponentially." Many years later, the Holy Spirit gave me a dream of a mathematical problem to help me understand the in-depth meaning of this prophecy.

THE DREAM

I dreamed I was trying to figure out a math problem involving multiplying numbers with exponents. The numbers were $100^{121} \times 100^{1234}$.

I could not remember the rules of how to multiply these numbers, and then I woke up.

ANALYSIS AND INTERPRETATION OF THE DREAM

I immediately began to think about the rules that apply when you multiply exponents with the same base number (100), and I remembered that you add the exponents when the base numbers (100) are the same. Of course, this number would be too large to be displayed on a calculator or an ordinary computer. The Holy Spirit interjected, "I don't want you to think about the rules of multiplying exponents. What I want you to understand is that I'm going to give you increase exponentially."

Exponential increase represents the expansion of spiritual and intellectual capacity. Holy Spirit used the prophecy from the math teacher and the mathematical problem to illustrate that He was increasing my capacity to develop problem-solving skills. I would be able to assess a problem within a community and work with others to provide a solution.

Holy Spirit can use dreams and visions to prepare us to become distribution centers and problem solvers like Joseph. Joseph used agricultural technology to continue to provide for the Egyptians when they no longer had money to purchase grain. He bought them and their land for Pharaoh when they no longer had anything to exchange to sustain their families. Joseph not only gave them seed for bread, but he also created jobs for them by giving them seed to plant the fields. He also gave them the right to keep four-fifths of the seed harvested to sustain their families and replant the fields. However, they were required to give one-fifth of the seed harvested to Pharoah (see Genesis 47:13–19). God had not only prepared Joseph for a position of power, but he also expanded Joseph's spiritual and intellectual capacity throughout his journey in Egypt. Pharoah acknowledged that God had given Joseph insight and wisdom when he approved of Joseph's plan to save Egypt from famine.

> So the advice was good in the eyes of Pharaoh and in the eyes of all his servants. And Pharaoh said to his servants, "Can we find *such a one* as this, a man in whom *is* the Spirit of God?" Then Pharaoh said to Joseph, "Inasmuch as God has shown you all this, *there is* no one as discerning and wise as you. You shall be over my house, and all my people shall be ruled according to your word; only in regard to the throne will I be greater than you." And Pharaoh said to Joseph, "See, I have set you over all the land of Egypt" (Genesis 41: 37–39 NKJV).

JOSEPH'S DOUBLE DREAM

Joseph's spiritual expansion began with two dreams that revealed his destiny before being sold into slavery and taken to Egypt (see Genesis 37:18–36). In the first dream, he saw his brothers' sheaves of wheat bowing down to his sheaf. When he told them about the dream, they asked him if he shall rule over them and have authority over them? In Joseph's second dream, he saw the sun, the moon, and the eleven stars bowing down to him. When he told his brothers and father about the second dream, his father asked him shall he, his mother, and his brothers bow down to him? (see Genesis 37:5–10).

Joseph's double dream manifested in its totality after his brothers were sent to Egypt for grain. The famine had reached their home country. Joseph had become the governor over all of Egypt, and his brothers had to bow before him before addressing him concerning their grain purchase. "And the sons of Israel went to buy *grain* among those who journeyed, for the famine was in the land of Canaan. Now Joseph *was* governor over the land; and it was he who sold to all the people of the land. And Joseph's brothers came and bowed down before him with *their* faces to the earth" (Genesis 42:5–7 NKJV).

God used Joseph to save his family and the lives of countless others from the famine. God will increase our spiritual and intellectual capacity to solve problems; however, the primary purpose of increasing our spiritual and intellectual capacity is to understand God's heart and mind. Understanding the heart and mind of God aligns our thoughts with God's will, the Scriptures, and His purpose for our lives. The following prayer reveals how one's spiritual and intellectual capacity can increase by praying to be filled with the wisdom, understanding, and knowledge needed to fulfill the will of God.

> For this reason, since the day we heard about it, we have not stopped praying for you, asking [specifically] that you may be filled with the *knowledge* of His will in all spiritual *wisdom* [with insight into His purposes], and in *understanding* [of spiritual things], so that you will walk in a manner worthy of the Lord

[displaying admirable character, moral courage, and personal integrity], to [fully] please Him in all things, bearing fruit in every good work and steadily growing in the knowledge of God [with deeper faith, clearer insight and fervent love for His precepts]; [we pray that you may be strengthened and invigorated with all power. (Colossians 1:9–11 AMP, emphasis added)

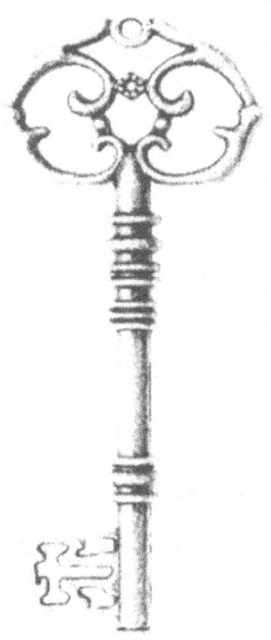

CHAPTER 11
DOORS IN YOUR MIND

The mind is a mystery. It is defined as "the element of a person that enables them to be aware of the world and their experiences, to think, and to feel; the faculty of consciousness and thought." The Holy Spirit revealed to me, "There are doors in your mind that lead to rooms in my heart (the mind and heart are connected). According to Dr. Cindy Trimm, the heart is the second compartment of the mind. She also stated that the mind is not one-dimensional but has five dimensions: the God-conscious, world-conscious, conscious, subconscious, and unconscious. Dr. Trimm also stated that the conscious mind operates by five senses (taste, touch, smell, sight, and hearing).

Dreams profoundly affect the subconscious mind. *The Cambridge English Dictionary* defines the subconscious as "the part of your mind that notices and remembers information when you are not actively trying to do so and influences your behavior even though you do not realize it." The Word of God has the same power in dreams to renew and transform our minds and hearts as it does in our everyday lives when we meditate on it.

In 1839, Edgar Allen Poe wrote an essay called "An Opinion on Dreams." He stated, "Dreams are a powerful form of consciousness: That dreams, or, as they were then generally called, visions, were a means of supernatural instruction, if we believe the Bible at all, is proved by Jacob's dream, the several visions of Ezekiel and other prophets, as also of later date, the Revelations to Saint John, and there appears no reason why this mode of divine communication should be discontinued in the present day." Note in Edgar Allen Poe's essay, he says that dreams, in general, were referred to as visions. However, not all visions mentioned in the Bible, as with Ezekiel and John (the Revelator), are dreams; they are a mode of transportation into the spiritual realm. In Revelation 4, John said that a door to heaven was opened unto him, and immediately he was in the spirit. His intimate connection with the Holy Spirit gave him access to the spiritual realm where he saw the throne of God (see Revelation 4:1–3).

EZEKIEL'S DOOR

In the book of Ezekiel, Ezekiel describes an unusual encounter with the Holy Spirit. He was transported by a vision into the spiritual realm to Jerusalem. Ezekiel was brought to the door of the temple's inner gate; he observed that an idol and the glory of God were present. His experience was taking place between earth and heaven in the second heaven.

> And it came to pass in the sixth year, in the sixth month, in the fifth day of the month, as I sat in mine house, and the elders of Judah sat before me, that the hand of the Lord GOD fell there upon me. Then I beheld, and lo a likeness as the appearance of fire: from the appearance of his loins even downward, fire; and from his loins even upward, as the appearance of brightness, as the colour of amber. And he put forth the form of an hand, and took me by a lock of mine head; and the spirit lifted me up between the earth and the heaven, and brought me in the visions of God to Jerusalem, to the door of the inner gate that looketh toward the north; where was the seat of the image of jealousy, which provoketh to jealousy. And, behold, the glory of the God of Israel was there, according to the vision that I saw in the plain. (Ezekiel 8:1–4)

As the vision continued, Ezekiel was led to the temple's court's door, saw a hole in a wall, and was instructed by the Spirit of God to dig through the wall. He discovered a door behind the wall. Ezekiel was going to receive intimate knowledge concerning the religious practices of the elders of the house of Israel. The Lord asked Ezekiel a very thought-provoking question, "Hast thou seen what the ancients of the house of Israel do in the dark, every man in the chambers of his imagery?" According to *Merriam Webster's Dictionary*, the definition of imagery is "mental images; especially the products of imagination." The imagination is a function of the mind; the "chambers of his imagery" refer to the rooms in the minds or hearts of the priests. God asked Ezekiel if he had seen what was going on in the imagination of the elders of the House of Israel? All truth is parallel, meaning what is true in the spirit is true in the natural. Ezekiel observed the vain imaginations of the priests' minds and what had been cultivated in their hearts, the strange pictures of idols and creatures on the walls of the temple.

> And he brought me to the door of the court; and when I looked, behold a hole in the wall. Then said he unto me, Son of man, dig now in the wall: and when I had digged in the wall, behold a door. And he said unto me, Go in, and behold the wicked abominations that they do here. So I went in and saw; and behold every form of creeping things, and abominable beasts, and all the idols of the house of Israel, pourtrayed upon the wall round about. And there stood before them seventy men of the ancients of the house of Israel…every man his censer in his hand; and a thick cloud of incense went up. Then said he unto me, Son of man, hast thou seen what the ancients of the house of Israel do in the dark, every man in the chambers of his imagery? for they

say, the LORD seeth us not; the LORD hath forsaken the earth. (Ezekiel 8:7–12)

Ezekiel observed the effect of idolatry on the minds and hearts of worshippers as he moved through the temple's various doors from the inner gate. He observed the worsening of defilement in these men's hearts and minds as he walked through each door. The worship of false gods had consumed these men. Ezekiel entered into higher realms of revelation as he passed through each door. The Holy Spirit led Ezekiel through the following four doors:

1. The door of the inner gate (Ezekiel 8:3)
2. The door of the court (Ezekiel 8:7)
3. The door behind the wall (Ezekiel 8:8)
4. The door of the gate of the Lord's house (Ezekiel 8:16)

The walls of the seventy priests' hearts and minds became overwritten with abominations that expressed adoration for foreign gods. In the Old and New Testaments, God spoke of putting his law in the hearts and minds of his people. He is our God, and we are his people.

> But this shall be the covenant that I will make with the house of Israel; After those days, saith the LORD, I will put my law in their inward parts, and write it in their hearts; and will be their God, and they shall be my people. (Jeremiah 31:33)

> This is the covenant that I will make with them after those days, saith the Lord, I will put my laws into their hearts, and in their minds will I write them. (Hebrews 10:16)

What we think about the most can become implanted in our hearts. What has been embedded in our hearts influences our beliefs, thoughts, and decisions. Proverbs 23:7 states, "For as he thinketh in his heart, so is he…" We know that thoughts are a function of the mind; proverbs 23:7 refers to the mind-heart connection. We are the temple of God; the Spirit of God lives inside of us. We are the temple that was not made with hands. God created us to house His Spirit and to worship Him.

> God that made the world and all things therein, seeing that he is Lord of heaven and earth, dwelleth not in temples made with hands; Neither is worshipped with men's hands, as though he needed anything, seeing he giveth to all life, and breath, and all things. (Acts 17:24–25)

> Know ye not that ye are the temple of God, and that the Spirit of God dwelleth in you? (1 Corinthians 3:16)

WORSHIPPING THE CREATION AND NOT THE CREATOR

Holy Spirit led Ezekiel through a series of doors into the inner court of the Lord's house and allowed him to see twenty-five men who had defiled themselves and the temple through sun worship. These men had turned their backs on God. They had lost their fear or reverence for the Lord. "So He brought me into the inner court of the LORD's house; and there, at the door of the temple of the LORD, between the porch and the altar, *were* about twenty-five men with their backs toward the temple of the LORD and their faces toward the east, and they were worshiping the sun toward the east" (Ezekiel 8:16 NKJV).

The elders of the House of Israel were worshipping the sun. The Apostle Paul wrote about idolatry in the book of Romans. He revealed in the passage below what happens to an idol worshipper's mind and heart when they worship created things instead of the Creator.

> For since the creation of the world God's invisible qualities—his eternal power and divine nature—have been clearly seen, being understood from what has been made, so that people are without excuse. For although they knew God, they neither glorified him as God nor gave thanks to him, but their thinking became futile and their foolish hearts were darkened. Although they claimed to be wise, they became fools and exchanged the glory of the immortal God for images made to look like a mortal human being and birds and animals and reptiles. They exchanged the truth about God for a lie, and worshiped and served created things rather than the Creator—who is forever praised. Amen. (Romans 1:20–23, 25 NIV)

The article "The Origination of Sun Worship" identifies Babylon, an ancient city and system in the Bible, as "the mother of all false worship systems." The Israelites were taken captive in Egypt and then Babylon for idolatry. They may have adopted this practice of sun worship while in captivity.

> Sun worship became the dominant religion in all ancient civilizations, spreading from Mother Babylon to India, China, Africa, Greece, Rome, Mexico, South America, Egypt, and Europe. Historically, pagan Babylon worshipped the sun as a deity, and pagan religions also worshipped the invincible sun. The first day of the week, the most pre-eminent position in the week, was therefore given to the worship of the sun in the calendar of the ancients. Worshipping on Sunday goes back at least two thousand years before Christ…Babylon is the mother of all "harlot" religions and all the pagan abominations and false worship systems that exists on earth!

Idolatry is the result of false religions and teachings. Worshipping on Sunday has been associated with worshipping the sun. However, I will state the obvious; worshiping the one, true, living God on Sunday is not the same as worshiping the sun. In the following passage, the priests and the temple servants were among the Israelites in Babylon; this may explain their embracing of idolatry and sun worship. "So all of Israel was enrolled by genealogies; and they are written in the Book of the Kings of Israel. And Judah was carried away into exile to Babylon because of their unfaithfulness [to God]. Now the first [of the returned exiles] who lived [again] in their possessions in their cities were Israel, the priests, the Levites, and the Nethinim" (temple servants) (1 Chronicles 9:1–2 AMP).

Whoever or whatever we worship has the power to take up residence in our hearts and influence our belief systems and thoughts. Jesus gives us an invitation to have communion with Him when we open the door of our hearts to Him. Jesus Himself said, "Here I am! I stand at the door and knock. If anyone hears my voice and opens the door, I will come in and with that person, and they with me" (Revelation 3:20 NIV).

CHAPTER 12
AWAKENING TO UNDERSTANDING

My dream about being in a box taught me an awakening must sometimes come first before we are aware of the reality of our spiritual condition. Natural sleep, in and of itself, is healthy. All the cells in our body are most regenerated when we sleep. "Daily Health Magazine" states, "Regeneration is the most important function of our body. Most of the regeneration process takes place when we sleep. Sleep is when our bodies rebuild, regenerate, and repair. Inadequate deep sleep may be the main cause of different degenerative disease such as early or rapid aging. Appropriate sleep is, in fact, an anti-aging, life-lengthening, and a surreptitious to the spout of Youth!"

I once heard the Spirit of God say, "While you were sleeping." God can mend, renew, and repair our minds while we sleep. Healing is just as much for our minds as it is for our bodies.

People have been put to sleep with errors and false teachings. When I say "put to sleep," I mean made inactive to what is going on spiritually, lack discernment, and have become insensitive to the Holy Spirit. In the story of Snow White, a spell was placed on what she had eaten, the enchanted apple. She ate the poisoned apple and fell into a deep sleep, making her appear dead. Many eat enchanted apples whenever they hear and receive erroneous or false teachings.

A DREAM WITHIN A DREAM

I had a dream within a dream after having a telephone conversation. After I hung up the phone, I immediately fell asleep on my bed where I had been having the conversation. The conversation continued into my first dream. When I thought I had woken up, I had a second dream. I saw myself lying on my bed with a strange man lying next to me. I knew he wanted to hurt me, so I told him that I would not report him because I would not be able to identify him. I distracted him and ran to the door. I reached for the handle to open the door. My eyes zoomed in on a small piece of bubble wrap stuck in the door opposite the inner lock mechanism that kept the door from locking. Then I woke up from both dreams.

ANALYSIS AND INTERPRETATION OF A DREAM WITHIN A DREAM

The first dream reflects how our conversations can infiltrate our dreams. In the second dream, the bedroom has a dual representation. It represents the place where we can have intimacy with God in our dreams, become pregnant with innovative ideas, and birth solutions to systemic problems. The bedroom also represents the heart. Shockingly, I had given the enemy access to my heart. Dreaming of wakening up in bed with a stranger symbolizes the issues of my heart. I tolerated a lot of verbal abuse and disrespectful behavior from those I had helped. I repetitively vented to others instead of setting boundaries. "Do you not understand that whatever goes into the mouth passes into the stomach, and is eliminated? But whatever[word]comes out of the mouth comes from the heart, and this is what defiles and dishonors the man" (Matthew 15:17–18 AMP).

My unhealthy way of coping (repetitive venting) gave the enemy access to my heart. The bubble wrap stuck in the door that kept it from locking symbolizes unhealthy protective coping mechanisms, preventing me from receiving inner healing. I had to repent, forgive, pray, and set boundaries. "Set a guard, O LORD, over my mouth; Keep watch over the door of my lips [to keep me from speaking thoughtlessly]" (Psalm 141:3 AMP).

A dream within a dream can unlock information stored in the subconscious mind and reveal the health of our spiritual condition. In researching the meaning of a dream within a dream, I read an article by Ethan Green called "False Awakening: Dreaming About Waking Up." A false awakening is when you dream you have woken up but continue to dream; then you wake up into reality. Ethan Green discusses a process that occurs when you have a dream within a dream called sleep fragmentation. In the article, he states, "Your brain can be in more than one state of consciousness at once. So it's possible that the part of your brain responsible for dreaming and also that for consciousness are both active. This fragmentation could then lead to vivid dreaming of gaining consciousness and waking up."

Ethan Green's observation of fragmentation may explain the process you experience not only when you dream to maintain the health of your body and mind but when you have a spiritual dream. The mind and the brain may be experiencing different levels of consciousness simultaneously to help us understand the knowledge downloaded in the dream realm. The spirit, soul, and body (the brain) work together to receive the message communicated in the dream.

In an article titled, "What Actually Happens In Your Body And Brain While You Sleep," Dr. Carl W. Brazilian was interviewed. Under the section, "Sleep is prime time for learning" the following was written: "One of the most active parts of the body during sleep is the brain, Bazil says. There are pronounced changes in the electrical activity of the brain during sleep, which the evidence suggests is a result of the brain's trillions of nerve cells literally rewiring themselves. This rewiring, which happens during deep, slow-wave sleep, is how we process and are thus able to retain new information we may have learned throughout the day..." I love that a section of the article is titled "Sleep is a prime time for learning," and explains how the brain is rewiring itself during sleep. One of the primary purposes of spiritual or prophetic dreams is to receive revelatory knowledge that transforms our thought patterns. The revelatory knowledge released in dreams can educate and train you to think strategically.

Analyzing and researching a dream within a dream is an excellent example of why you are the best person to interpret your dreams. Dream analysis and interpretation can be therapeutic—bring health to your spirit, soul, and body. You can receive insight that activates inner healing, deliverance, and strategies to strengthen your inner self. The more time you spend communicating with the Holy Spirit concerning dreams and visions, the more you will understand how to utilize the information revealed in these encounters.

A VISION WITHIN A VISION

Once, I went into a trance and had a vision within a vision. This trance was not an induced state that some have reached through hypnosis or ungodly meditation. Those dangerous practices can expose you to the dark side of the spiritual realm and deceitful spiritual beings masquerading as spirit guides or teachers. The Holy Spirit opened the spiritual realm unto me to impart insight concerning my assignment.

I turned the light off in my bedroom and went to bed. Immediately, I saw myself standing in front of the sliding glass door that leads to my patio. The view from my patio is a man-made lake with three fountains. As I was standing there, I was thinking; that I needed to go to the bank for a childhood neighbor. As I looked out the sliding glass door leading to my patio, where the man-made lake and fountains should have been,

I saw a white car with a hood ornament. I heard the voice of God say, "This is not your father's car." I thought I had woken up from what appeared to be a dream. Then, I had a second vision, I saw myself standing on the side of my bed, and the light was on. I was clapping my hands and singing, "Oh, the blood of Jesus." Then I woke from the vision.

ANALYSIS AND INTERPRETATION OF A VISION WITHIN A VISION

In the first vision, my neighbor was a math and science teacher who greatly encouraged me as a child. She died almost ten years ago. I was thinking about going to the bank for my neighbor as I stared outside the sliding glass door. We usually go to the bank to deposit or withdraw money (make a transaction). We should never make any transactions on behalf of the dead. Sometimes when we dream about someone who has died, a demonic spirit (a spirit guide) is masquerading as one of our loved ones to get us to engage with it in the spiritual or dream realm so that it can interact with us in our waking hours. However, God can give you a dream about a loved one who has passed away to comfort and encourage you.

In the second vision, I see myself clapping and singing, Oh, the blood of Jesus represents praising God. I was praising God for justifying and sanctifying me for His purpose through Jesus's sacrifice on the cross. The lamp represents the Word of God. The lamp being on means walking in the spirit or being led by the Holy Spirit. The presence of light in the room represents God's glory (presence) and the nature of Christ (truth, holiness, and righteousness).

When I awoke from the vision within a vision, I began to think about what the voice of God said, *"This is not your father's car."* The Holy Spirit revealed to me that the car was an Oldsmobile. Oldsmobile had a slogan with a jingle. "This is not your father's car. This is the next generation . . ." The car's color (white) represents a ministry built on holiness and righteousness. This part of the vision highlighted a part of my purpose to teach the next generation about their identity, destiny, and kingdom principles—holiness and righteousness. It also signified that I would do things differently than other generations.

My experience illustrates being transported into the spirit realm via a vision within a vision. The purpose of this experience is to understand the importance of rejecting unhealthy traditions, ungodly ways, and all transactions with the kingdom of darkness. The experience illustrates that transformation (of the mind) comes from embracing God's Word and a life of holiness. It also confirmed my assignment to teach the gospel of the Kingdom through mentorships. The most important symbols in the two visions pointed me to the following Scriptures:

THE WHITE CAR: TRANSFORMATIONAL MINISTRY

1. Transformation of the heart and the mind allows us to model the nature of Christ (holy and righteous) to generations of people.

So prepare your minds for action, be completely sober [in spirit—steadfast, self-disciplined, spiritually and morally alert], fix your hope completely on the grace [of God] that is coming to you when Jesus Christ is revealed., [Live] as obedient children [of God]; do not be conformed to the evil desires which governed you in your ignorance [before you knew the requirements and transforming power of the good news regarding salvation]. But like the Holy One who called you, be holy yourselves in all your conduct [be set apart from the world by your godly character and moral courage]; because it is written, "You shall be holy (set apart), for I am holy." (1 Peter 1:13–16 AMP)

THE LAMP

2. When we embrace the Word of God, it will guide and direct us.

I have restrained my feet from every evil way, That I may keep Your word. I have not turned aside from Your ordinances, For You Yourself have taught me. How sweet are Your words to my taste, Sweeter than honey to my mouth! Through Your precepts I get understanding; Therefore I hate every false way. Your word is a lamp to my feet And a light to my path. (Psalm 119:101–105 NKJV)

LIGHT

3. When we follow Christ and reject ungodly thoughts, behaviors, practices, and lifestyles, we will reflect the nature of Christ.

This is the message which we have heard from Him and declare to you, that God is light and in Him is no darkness at all. If we say that we have fellowship with Him, and walk in darkness, we lie and do not practice the truth. But if we walk in the light as He is in the light, we have fellowship with one another, and the blood of Jesus Christ His Son cleanses us from all sin. (1 John 1:5–7 NKJV)

THE BLOOD OF JESUS

4. Transformation of the heart and mind begins with embracing the work completed on the cross when Jesus's blood was shed to justify and sanctify us.

And if under the old system the blood of bulls and goats and the ashes of young cows could cleanse men's bodies from sin, just think how much more surely the blood of Christ will transform our lives and hearts. His sacrifice frees us from the worry of having to obey the old rules and makes us want to serve the living God. For by the help of the eternal Holy Spirit, Christ willingly gave himself to God to die for our sins—he being perfect, without a single sin or fault. (Hebrew 9:13–14 TLB)

But God clearly shows *and* proves His own love for us, by the fact that while we were still sinners, Christ died for us. Therefore, since we have now been justified [declared free of the guilt of sin] by His blood, [how much more certain is it that] we will be saved from the wrath *of God* through Him. For if while we were enemies we were reconciled to God through the death of His Son, *it is* much more *certain*, having been reconciled, that we will be saved [from the consequences of sin] by His life [that is, we will be saved because Christ lives today]. (Romans 5:8–10)

PART III
THE KEYS

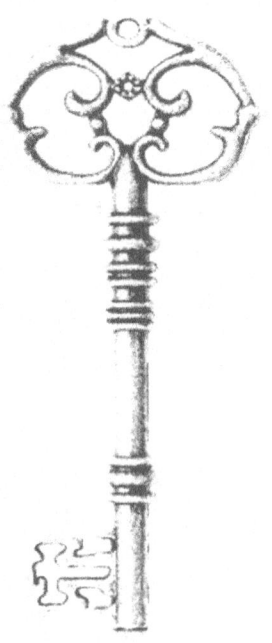

CHAPTER 13
THE KEYS OF THE KINGDOM

Dreaming of keys can signify being given an assignment or being empowered. Receiving keys in a dream can also mean receiving delegated governmental authority and power to fulfill the will of God on earth as it is heaven. We can exercise this authority and power by teaching and educating others about the kingdom of God. According to *Smith's Bible Dictionary*, "keys are used in Scripture as a symbol of authority and power. Giving keys to a person signifies the intrusting of him with an important charge." A charge is defined as the following: 1.) to command, instruct, or exhort with authority 2.) to impose a task or responsibility on.

THE HISTORY OF THE KEYS OF THE KINGDOM

The function of the keys of the kingdom is illustrated in Isaiah 22. The Key of the House of David is one of the most significant keys illustrating God's authority and power given to an obedient servant to govern God's kingdom on the earth. The Prophet Isaiah received the revelation concerning the Key of the House of David in the Valley of Vision. Isaiah was sent by God to the standing governor, "In that day I will call my servant Eliakim the son of Hilkiah, and I will clothe him with your robe, and will bind your sash on him, and will commit your authority to his hand. And he shall be a father to the inhabitants of Jerusalem and to the house of Judah. And I will place on his shoulder the key of the house of David. He shall open, and none shall shut; and he shall shut, and none shall open" (Isaiah 22:20–22 ESV).

Shebna's robe symbolizes the anointing, authority, and position (mantle) that Eliakim would receive. His sash symbolizes the strength and power that would be imparted to Eliakim. Eliakim, having the Key of the House of David placed upon his shoulder, represents being empowered to bear the responsibilities assigned to him by the king. The Key of the House of David being placed upon his shoulder is very significant because, according to *The KJV Dictionary*, the shoulder is defined as "Figuratively, support; sustaining power; or that which elevates and sustains." The Key of the House of David symbolizes having control over access to the king's house or kingdom.

Eliakim is a type and a shadow of Jesus, who now possesses the Key of David and controls access to the kingdom of God.

> "Let not your hearts be troubled. Believe in God; believe also in me. In my Father's house are many rooms. If it were not so, would I have told you that I go to prepare a place for you? And if I go and prepare a place for you, I will come again and will take you to myself, that where I am you may be also. And you know the way to where I am going." Thomas said to him, "Lord, we do not know where you are going. How can we know the way?" Jesus said to him, "I am the way, and the truth, and the life. *No one comes to the Father except through me.*" (John 14:1–6 ESV, emphasis added)

The New Testament introduction to the keys of the kingdom of heaven begins with Jesus questioning the disciples about His identity. He revealed to Peter, who answered correctly, that his revelation concerning His identity was given to him by God the Father, not human reasoning. Then, Jesus explained the function of the keys of the kingdom of heaven to the disciples.

> Simon Peter replied, "You are the Christ (the Messiah, the Anointed), the Son of the living God." Then Jesus answered him, "Blessed [happy, spiritually secure, favored by God] are you, Simon son of Jonah, because flesh and blood (mortal man) did not reveal this to you, but My Father who is in heaven. I will give you the keys (authority) of the kingdom of heaven; and

whatever you bind [forbid, declare to be improper and unlawful] on earth will have [already] been bound in heaven, and whatever you loose [permit, declare lawful] on earth will have [already] been loosed in heaven." (Matthew 16:16–17, 19 AMP)

It is important to understand the scriptural purpose of the keys. The above passage tells us the keys of the kingdom of heaven have the power to bind (forbid, declare to be improper and unlawful) and loose (permit, declare lawful). The keys of the kingdom are exercised through the teaching of the gospel of the kingdom. According to *The Cambridge Bible for Schools and Colleges Commentary* on Matthew 16:19, *the keys of the kingdom of heaven*—"This expression was not altogether new. To a Jew it would convey a definite meaning. He would think of the symbolic key given to a Scribe when admitted to his office, with which he was to open the treasury of the divine oracles. Peter was to be a Scribe in the kingdom of heaven. He has received authority to teach the truths of the kingdom."

Jesus used the word "keys" to describe the authority He gave Peter and the other disciples to teach and see the will of God be done on earth as it is in heaven. Peter's revelation unlocked the revelation for all of the disciples on how to receive the keys of the kingdom of heaven by knowing Christ's identity and knowing Him intimately. Apostle John Eckhardt states the following in his book *The Invisible King and His Kingdom*: "The keys of the kingdom represent the authority of the kingdom. Keys give access. Keys open and close doors. The authority of the kingdom was given unto Peter because of a revelation. Those who have this revelation have authority. The authority of the kingdom is based on revelation. Those who walk in kingdom power and authority are those who have revelation."

THE KEY OF KNOWLEDGE

Another important key is called the key of knowledge. This key is also a kingdom key and illustrates how the keys of the kingdom function. The key of knowledge gave access to revelation concerning the kingdom of heaven. Jesus discussed the key of knowledge with the professors of the Law, who attempted to impede and bar the gospel of the kingdom of heaven. "'Woe to you lawyers, because you have taken away the key to knowledge (scriptural truth). You yourselves did not enter, and you held back those who were entering [by your flawed interpretation of God's word and your man-made tradition]'" (Luke 11:52 AMP).

Ellicott's Commentary for English Readers discusses how the key of knowledge illustrates that truth could be withheld from everyday people. Those authorized to interpret and read Scriptures possessed a physical key to access "the treasurer chamber of the interpreter." The scribes withheld knowledge to access the kingdom of heaven. The withholding of this information also kept the people from accessing greater truth stored in heavenly realms that would cause them to receive the greatest form of transformation—salvation. If we are willing to pray and study the Word of God, the Holy Spirit will begin to teach us what others have attempted to withhold from us and more. The knowledge that the Holy Spirit unveils goes far beyond man's knowledge.

Woe unto you, lawyers! —The "woe" in this case is uttered against those who were, by their very calling, the professed interpreters of the Law. Its form rests on the fact that each scribe or "doctor of the law," in the full sense of the term, was symbolically admitted to his office by the delivery of a key. His work was to enter with that key into the treasure-chambers of the house of the interpreter and to bring forth thence "things new and old" (Matthew 13:52). The sin of the "lawyers" of that time, the "divines" as we should call them, was that they claimed a monopoly of the power to interpret, and yet did not exercise the power.

Jesus contended with the interpreters of the Law by teaching the mysteries of the kingdom of heaven in parables. The Prophet Isaiah prophesied that Jesus would teach in parables. "All these things Jesus said to the crowds in parables; indeed, he said nothing to them without a parable. This was to fulfill what was spoken by the prophet: 'I will open my mouth in parables; I will utter what has been hidden since the foundation of the world'" (Matthew 13:34–35 ESV).

Parables are a pattern of teaching used in the Old and New Testaments to unlock mysteries hidden in the Scriptures. *The Prophet's Dictionary* defines a parable as "An earthly or natural example used allegorically to demonstrate or express heaven's spiritual truths. Parables usually take the form of short stories that use figures of speech to communicate their spiritual and eternal principles...As a result, they are highly illustrative and draw on everyday life details common to the hearer." In the New Testament, this type of instruction would become known as the teachings of Jesus Christ or the gospel of the kingdom.

> O my people, listen to my instructions. Open your ears to what I am saying, for I will speak to you in a parable. I will teach you hidden lessons from our past—stories we have heard and known, stories our ancestors handed down to us. We will not hide these truths from our children; we will tell the next generation about the glorious deeds of the LORD, about his power and his mighty wonders. For he issued his laws to Jacob; he gave his instructions to Israel. He commanded our ancestors to teach them to their children, so the next generation might know them—even the children not yet born—and they in turn will teach their own children. (Psalm 78:1–6 NLT)

Holy Spirit is our teacher, just as Jesus was the master or teacher of the disciples when He walked the earth. Holy Spirit will give us revelation when we read the Bible. Look at this powerful quote from Horace Greeley concerning those who read their Bible. "It is impossible to enslave, mentally or socially, a Bible-reading people. The principles of the Bible are the groundwork of human freedom."

We should study and verify that what is being taught to us is scriptural. Verifying that a teaching is scriptural is another way to gain revelatory knowledge. Acts 17:11 states, "These were more noble than those in Thessalonica, in that they received the word with all readiness of mind, and searched the Scriptures daily, whether those things were so."

THE MASTER'S KEY: THE KEY OF DAVID

The governmental authority that God had granted David to rule a kingdom was transferred to David's royal lineage (i.e., Solomon and Jesus). Jesus having the Key of David signifies he has been given all power and authority over the kingdom of God. According to an article titled, *What Is the Key of David?* "The Key of David is a term found in Revelation and Isaiah. A key indicates control or authority; therefore, having the Key of David would give one control of David's domain, i.e., Jerusalem, the City of David, and the kingdom of Israel. The fact that, in Revelation 3:7, Jesus holds this key shows that He is the fulfillment of the Davidic Covenant, the ruler of the New Jerusalem, and the Lord of the kingdom of heaven."

Men who possessed the key of knowledge would no longer be able "to shut up heaven" or prevent people from being able to enter into the kingdom of heaven by withholding knowledge. Salvation grants us entrance into the kingdom of God. The letter the Lord instructed the Apostle John (the Revelator) to write to the church of Philadelphia confirms that Jesus has authority over access into the kingdom of God. "'He who has an ear, let him hear what the Spirit says to the churches.' 'And to the angel of the church in Philadelphia write, These things says He who is holy, He who is true, 'He who has the key of David, He who opens and no one shuts, and shuts and no one opens': 'I know your works. See, I have set before you an open door, and no one can shut it; for you have a little strength, have kept My word, and have not denied My name'" (Revelation 3:6–8 NKJV).

The Key of David is important to us as believers today because it represents access to the throne of God in heaven through the understanding of the Scriptures. The governmental authority that David and his sons carried came from their ability to unlock multiple dimensions of revelation stored within the Scriptures. According to an article written by Homer Kizer titled, *The Key of David*, the Key of David functions as follows:

> The Key of David is the key that unlocks Scripture: it means understanding the writings of King David, a man after God's heart, a man who used the outside/inside movement of the Hebraic poetics to simultaneously reveal and conceal knowledge. David's use of repetition to form couplets within David's songs, a poetic style he inherited, functions to marry the visible to the invisible, thereby causing the visible to become a copy and shadow of the invisible (Hebrews 8:5 et al.). The Key of David uses typology to unlock sealed and secret prophecies, to reveal the mysteries of God, and to hide these secret things of God from the natural nation of Israel that saw only with eyes and heard only with ears.

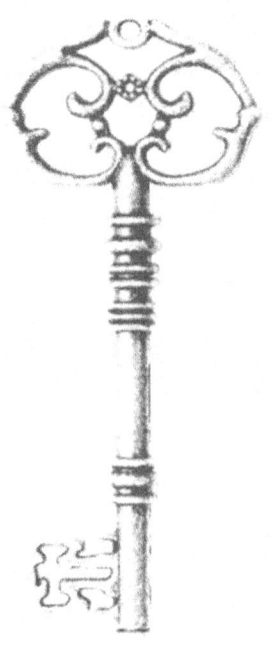

CHAPTER 14
SPIRITUAL IDENTITY

Our purpose, call, and job titles describe our responsibilities; they are not our spiritual identity. Our spiritual identity is birthed out of our relationship with God the Father through Jesus Christ and the work of the Holy Spirit. There are different degrees of relationship that we can have with the Lord. When we receive salvation, we become the children of God and receive a spiritual inheritance—eternal life and access to the kingdom of God. We become heirs of God and citizens of the kingdom of God. If we are obedient to the Holy Spirit, we are the sons of God—this is our spiritual identity (see 8:14–17 AMP).

SLAVE MENTALITY, SOUL TIES, AND OUR IDENTITY

It is in oppressive and controlling environments where a slave mentality can be developed and suppress a person's spiritual identity. In these environments, people are conditioned to believe that they are incapable of critical thinking and making quality decisions without a person in a position of authority's approval. Anyone who has been in an atmosphere where the leadership is abusive, no matter our background, financial status, or title, can become susceptible to oppressive ideas when we do not know the truth or our spiritual identity. A dear friend told me, "Sometimes people have a slave mentality and need someone to pray them out of it. They have trouble thinking for themselves because of the slave mentality."

A soul tie can develop when we have an attachment to someone to fill a void in our lives. I developed an emotional bond with a spiritual leader; it created a false sense of obligation and responsibility towards them. I prayed and severed the emotional attachment I had developed with this person. We can learn to walk in the freedom that Jesus has purchased for us through His blood, shed on the cross without emotional manipulation, shame or guilt. "You were bought at a price; do not become slaves of men" (1 Corinthians 7:23 NKJV).

DREAMS OF DELIVERANCE

Harriet Tubman, later known as "Black Moses," grew up in a slavery system but did not have a slave mentality. Slave mentality is often taught and fostered by the atmospheres and environments influencing our lives. Harriet Tubman led many who had been enslaved physically, mentally, emotionally, and spiritually to freedom, just as Moses had done with the children of Israel when they were delivered from Egypt. Living inside these systems prepared Moses and Harriet Tubman to receive the instructions to lead people to freedom. Some of Harriet Tubman's instructions to gain her freedom and lead others to freedom came from dreams and visions.

RELEASE FROM A FALSE IDENTITY

Some people, including myself, have taken on false identities because of lies. One time, I had a dream, I was sitting in the passenger's seat of a car, and the driver said to me, "Son of lies." I replied, "Son of lies?" Then I woke up.

ANALYSIS AND INTERPRETATION OF THE DREAM

Who was the person sitting in the driver's seat? The Holy Spirit, the Spirit of truth, was sitting in the driver's seat. Why was I sitting in the passenger's seat? Being in the passenger's seat symbolizes my submission to the Holy Spirit and His guidance. He was revealing to me the truth about how lies are conceived. "When the Spirit of truth comes, he will guide you into all truth. He will not speak on his own but will tell you what he has heard. He will tell you about the future" (John 16:13 NLT).

What does "son of lies" mean? "Son of lies" is symbolic of the work conceived by Satan and points to an explanation of how Satan, "the father of lies," can infiltrate the heart and minds of people. "You belong to your father, the devil, and you want to carry out your father's desires. He was a murderer from the beginning, not holding to the truth, for there is no truth in him. When he lies, he speaks his native language, for he is a liar and the father of lies" (John 8:44 NIV).

Many unhealthy perceptions and behaviors can be birthed out of a lie spiritually. In the same way, a baby is created; they are conceived. The following passage illustrates this. "When tempted, no one should say, 'God is tempting me.' For God cannot be tempted by evil, nor does he tempt anyone; but each person is tempted when they are dragged away by their own evil desire and enticed. Then, after desire has conceived, it gives birth to sin; and sin, when it is full-grown, gives birth to death" (James 1:13–15 NIV). Once we have embraced a lie in our hearts and minds, it can produce distorted thoughts of ourselves and our self-worth.

During this time, I was learning how to live outside of the box—how to think for myself. I had allowed people to control and influence me to embrace a false identity birthed out of lies and an inferiority complex. One of those lies is that when you begin to think for yourself and reject people's toxic behavior in a position of authority in the church, you have become rebellious and disobedient—you don't want anybody telling you what to do. It is important to have pastors, teachers, spiritual leaders, and mentors in our lives who can give us godly counsel and education.

Years ago, the Lord told me to tell people, "There is a (loving, intimate) relationship that I want to have with you that is sometimes misrepresented in church." God loves you and desires to have a relationship with you. Do not keep allowing the father of lies to torment you. God is willing and able to set you free from the hurt and the shame that may have come from toxic relationships associated with church.

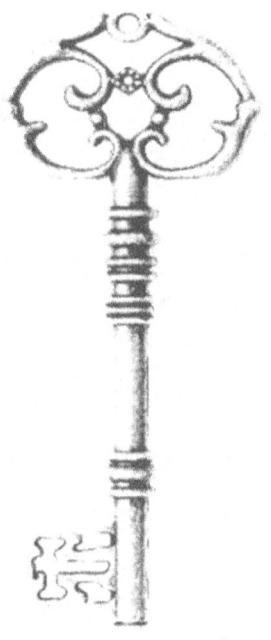

CHAPTER 15
REVELATORY KEYS AND MYSTERIES

For the last fifteen years, I have dreamt more about keys than anything else. God gave me dreams about different types of keys to teach me about the different dimensions and functions of authority. These keys symbolized being given authority and power to unlock revelatory knowledge that can bring transformation to our minds, families, and communities through biblical education concerning the kingdom of God. It is not enough to know that there are many different types of keys—authority and power available to believers. It is imperative to pray and understand how these keys function.

Once, I stayed in a beautiful Hilton hotel by the ocean. I received another type of key; a room key card with a prophetic slogan on its key cardholder. I was in awe when I read the slogan on the room key card-holder: "Open doors that you never knew existed." It inspired me to think about the different types of keys given to me in dreams and to understand how they work. What kind of doors do they open?

KEYS THAT UNLOCK REVELATION

I dreamt of standing outside with a group of people, and only some of us received a key. I felt terrible for a woman who did not receive a key, but I knew I needed it to be able to go to the next place. I found a locked black box, and when I opened it, another key was inside.

ANALYSIS AND INTERPRETATION OF THE DREAM

The people who received keys, including myself, represent people called to the office of a teacher; we teach by revelation imparted to us by the Holy Spirit. The two keys that I received represent access to revelatory knowledge. The key in the locked black box represents something hidden, concealed, or secret. The color black has multiple meanings, but in this dream it symbolizes mysteries. I was given authority to unlock the understanding of mysteries. How did I know where the box was? I was led by the Holy Spirit to its location, although I did not know what the box contained. This dream represents revelatory knowledge that can only be unlocked with other revelatory knowledge. The more we grow in our understanding of the Word of God, the more opportunity or access we will be given to unlock revelation. Once the mind is opened, we can continually receive more understanding to elevate our thinking. "However, as it is written: 'What no eye has seen, what no ear has heard, and what no human mind has conceived'—the things God has prepared for those who love him—these are the things God has revealed to us by his Spirit. The Spirit searches all things, even the deep things of God" (1 Corinthians 2:9–10 NIV).

When I began to reanalyze this dream, the Holy Spirit brought to my remembrance a Scripture that He had spoken to my spirit in the year 2000: "I will give you the treasures of darkness, and riches hidden in secret places..." (Isaiah 45:3). He told me that this verse refers to mysteries; I decided to do a word study on the phrase *treasures of darkness*. Word studies can also help you determine the interpretation of a dream and unlock revelatory knowledge. I read this article titled, *Word Study-Treasure of Darkness*, and it says that the treasure in Isaiah 45:3 is knowledge, and darkness refers to something being hidden. This word study defined the treasures of darkness as "the deep mysteries of God stored away in His Word."

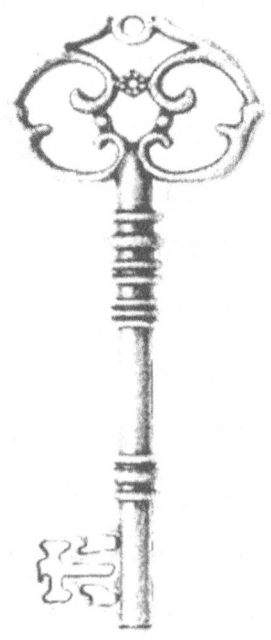

CHAPTER 16
MANTLES

Clothing in a dream can represent a mantle: the anointing, authority, and position God has given a believer to fulfill an assignment. Jesus clothes or mantles us when we embrace Him as our Savior. In the following passage, "clothed" explains how God has covered us with salvation and His righteousness when we enter into a relationship with the Lord. The Lord clothing us with a robe of righteousness also describes how He has given us a position in the kingdom of God and anoints us to share the gospel of the kingdom.

> The Spirit of the Sovereign LORD is upon me, for the LORD has anointed me to bring good news to the poor. He has sent me to comfort the brokenhearted and to proclaim that captives will be released and prisoners will be freed. (Isaiah 61:1 NLT)

> I am overwhelmed with joy in the LORD my God! For he has dressed me with the clothing of salvation and draped me in a robe of righteousness. I am like a bridegroom dressed for his wedding or a bride with her jewels. (Isaiah 61:10 NLT)

THE DREAM MANTLE

A mantle that the Holy Spirit has given to a believer can be revealed in a dream. I had a dream that one of my former pastors was standing at a door holding a white robe neatly folded in a clear package. She asked me, "Do you have one of these?" My dream shifted, and the two of us were sitting, facing each other on two twin beds. The white robe now appeared as a dark blue, long nightshirt covered with stars and crescent-shaped moons. She tossed it up, and it went on my head. As soon as I awoke, I asked the Holy Spirit, "What did you just show me?" The Holy Spirit answered, "the dream mantle." I had never heard of this kind of mantle before.

ANALYSIS AND INTERPRETATION OF THE DREAM

The white robe represents holiness and righteousness given to the believer. The transformation of the robe into a nightshirt with stars and moons illustrates the divine tailoring of the mantle God places on our lives to fulfill our purpose and assignment. Tossing the nightshirt onto my head was symbolic of receiving wisdom, understanding, and knowledge; my mind would be transformed. The moons and stars represent light—revelation given in the night hours in dreams. The nightshirt represents Joseph's mantle as a dreamer, an interpreter of dreams, a problem solver, and a strategist who could receive wisdom through dreams and visions. My former pastor and I sitting on twin beds meant that we are both dreamers, have similar anointings and spiritual gifts.

This dream taught me that the Holy Spirit can appear in the likeness of a person that has a particular mantle or gift so that you can identify what will be or has been imparted to you. Yes, this dream is the inspiration for the main title of this series, *The Dream Mantle*. The dream revealed that I had been given an anointing and authority to help transform families, communities, systems, and nations. After this dream, I began having more complex dreams: dreams within dreams, a series of dreams, and visions within dreams. A series of dreams is when you are dreaming and have two dreams that appear to be separate, but they are one dream; the second dream is a continuation of the first dream.

THE DREAM

I had a dream that I was sitting in a restaurant in a beautiful resort with large picture windows. As I looked out the window, I saw an astronaut walking on the beach with his helmet under his arm. He was walking towards the restaurant. The ocean was behind him. Twenty-five silk robes shaped in a half-circle were lying on the beach. Then my view shifted, and I was looking at Asian people wearing silk robes, sitting at the base of a hill. At the top of the hill was a large statue with a long mustache and beard. He was wearing a hat with a tassel.

ANALYSIS AND INTERPRETATION OF THE DREAM

Sitting at the table in the dream represents being prepared to spiritually consume or receive wisdom and knowledge. To interpret what looking out the large picture window meant, I thought about its natural function. A window allows light to enter into a place and represents receiving revelation or illumination of the mind to produce transformation. The window's size was also important because it allowed me to have an unobstructed view of what was taking place on the beach. The astronaut represents a person with authority in heaven and the earth realm. According to *The Divinity Code to Understanding Your Dreams and Visions*, an astronaut can represent the following:

1. Jesus
2. A spiritual person raised up
3. In the place of authority

The twenty-five silk robes represent mantles. There are mantles for specific regions and countries. A mantle can be given to a person to complete an assignment. *The Divinity Code to Understanding Your Dreams and Visions* defines a mantle as "a spiritual authority, the anointing, covering, spiritual position or office." The number twenty-five means God's grace and redemption. The mantles are for those who have been chosen to teach the kingdom of God in Asia. These people will bring transformation to Asia. When they receive the mantle, they will receive power and authority to minister with miracles, signs, and wonders. In the Bible, Jesus sent the apostles to preach the kingdom of God throughout the world. "Then he called his twelve disciples together, and gave them power and authority over all devils, and to cure diseases. And he sent them to preach the kingdom of God, and to heal the sick" (Luke 9:1–2).

The people sitting at the bottom of the hill below the statue were worshipping. They represent people who will be transformed by the teaching of the gospel of the kingdom. They too, will bring transformation to the communities they live in and nations.

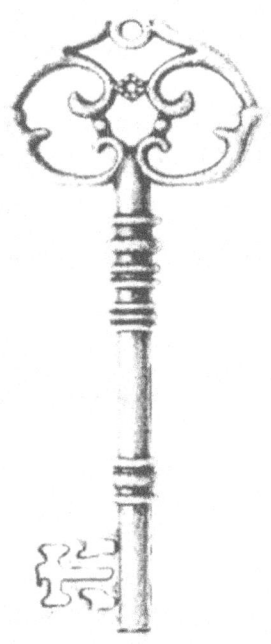

CHAPTER 17
UNLOCKING UNDERSTANDING

Getting out of the box or allowing your frame of mind to be changed to the will of God removes ceilings and walls. Ceilings and walls are representations of limitations and barriers. Transformation of the mind helps us expand our knowledge base, be more receptive to Holy Spirit's guidance, and release our creativity. It also elevates us in understanding our purpose and identity in the kingdom of God. It took years for me to learn that getting out of the box is a process because it requires changing our thought processes through renewing our minds with the Word of God. Getting out of the box also requires healing and deliverance from false teaching and oppressive religious practices.

After I had the dream of getting out of the box, I began to have dreams about doors being opened for me into new international territories, assignments, and different realms of God's glory. I also started dreaming of receiving a limitless supply of the anointing for healing, deliverance, and breakthroughs. I began to travel and assist with global missions work more frequently in the places I had dreamt.

THE DREAM

I had a dream that I was sitting on my bed in my room. There were no doors in the room. The room was well lit. I was staring at the wall that my television is mounted on, but there was no television. The wall had this substance that looked like lard or fat caked on it. Then, I noticed that oil was streaming down the wall. Then I woke up.

ANALYSIS AND INTERPRETATION OF THE DREAM

The wall represents a barrier. One definition of a barrier is a "anything that restrains or obstructs progress, access, etc." The substance that appeared like lard or fat represents a heavy anointing, and the flowing oil represents the anointing that has been released in my life for breakthroughs. *The Prophet's Dictionary* defines anointing oil as "An applied substance made from olives or other vegetables used for food, healing, and light…The practice signified induction into divine service, making anointing oil's common uses classified as spiritual nourishment, spiritual and supernatural healing, impartation of empowerment for office, and revelatory enlightenment for wisdom."

In the natural realm, on the right and left sides of the wall are entryways that lead to doors that lead to a hallway. In my dream, these entryways did not exist. In dreams, entryways represent access, doors represent opportunities, and hallways represent transition. No television represents no influence from the outside world. Sitting on the bed signified receiving revelatory knowledge released through dreams to bring breakthroughs. The absence of the television, entryways, and doors magnified the significance of what was in the room:

1. The Holy Spirit
2. The anointing
3. Light: illumination of the mind, instructions, knowledge

This dream's message is that there is a barrier-breaking anointing available, and it gives us access to different realms of God's Glory, where wisdom and revelation exist. The definition of a breakthrough is "A sudden, dramatic, and important discovery or development." The anointing will help us to unlock creative and innovative ideas.

The anointing can release us from spiritual and man-made barriers designed to keep us from the presence of God. The anointing carries the power to liberate us from spiritual and physical bondage. Israel spent years in physical captivity because of idolatry. Isaiah 10 talks about God delivering Israel from their Assyrian oppressors because of the anointing. He describes this anointing as having the power to remove burdens and destroy yokes. *The KJV Dictionary* defines yoke as "A mark of servitude, slavery or bondage. Note that the word *anointing* in the King James Version is fat in the Amplified Version. Look at the two different translations of Isaiah 10:27.

1. And it shall come to pass in that day, that his burden shall be taken away from off thy shoulder, and his yoke from off thy neck, and the yoke shall be destroyed because of the anointing. (KJV)

2. So it will be in that day, that the burden of the Assyrian will be removed from your shoulders and his yoke from your neck. The yoke will be broken because of the fat. (AMP)

THE SPIRIT OF UNDERSTANDING

I know that praying to have a spirit of understanding activated an increase of spiritual dreams in my life. Studying and meditating on Scriptures enhanced my understanding of complex prophetic dreams that unlock our spiritual identity, destiny, and capacity. "I thought, 'Ages should speak; advanced years should teach wisdom.' But it is the spirit in a person, the breath of the Almighty, that gives them understanding" (Job 32:7–8 NIV).

THE DREAM

I once had a dream that I was working in a hospital. It was time to go home, so I got in the elevator with a short black woman; I thought she was a nurse. I pushed the elevator button to go to the 1st floor, and the elevator went to the 39th floor and then to the 144th floor. When I went to the 144th floor, I noticed a man with shoulder-length gray hair wearing glasses. He was holding a clear glass of water. I took a sip of the glass of water. There was also a woman in the elevator, holding a brown, boat-shaped glass dish with a light blue, silver glaze. She was not the same woman I was initially with when I first got on the elevator. It reminded me of a candy dish from the 1970s. The dish appeared to be full of iced tea and ice cubes. I took a large gulp of what I thought was iced tea. It was hot sweet tea, and it tasted awful, like it had liquid plastic in it. When I woke up, the memory of the terrible taste of the hot sweet tea and plastic lingered as though I still tasted it.

ANALYSIS AND INTERPRETATION OF THE DREAM

The elevator represents spiritual elevation. Going to the 39th floor and then to the 144th floor represents transcending multiple levels in the spiritual realm. Stopping at the 39th floor represents how the Holy Spirit allows us time to adjust to the new altitudes He takes us to in the spiritual realm. What about the woman that was in the elevator with me? She was an angel assigned to accompany and protect me as I traveled through unfamiliar levels in the spiritual realm. I have seen angels before in my dreams dressed as nurses, police officers, and flight attendants.

In the dream, I wanted to go to the 1st floor to go home. When the elevator began to ascend to the 39th floor, I had an unusual amount of peace; the amount of peace that I had, represents my receptiveness to go wherever the Lord takes me, even in the spiritual realm. Initially, I began to look up what the number 39 symbolized. I realized the act of going to the 39th floor was what needed to be interpreted. What appeared to be the end of a normal workday was the beginning of a spiritual experience designed to educate, activate, and elevate my understanding of biblical principles, such as the following:

1. God has given us the Holy Spirit as a teacher and not the spirit that the world is guided by.

Now we have received, not the spirit of the world, but the [Holy] Spirit who is from God, so that we may know *and* understand the [wonderful] things freely given to us by God. (1 Corinthians 2:12 AMP)

2. Spiritual things can only be understood as the Holy Spirit reveals them.

But the natural [unbelieving] man does not accept the things [the teachings and revelations] of the Spirit of God, for they are foolishness [absurd and illogical] to him; and he is incapable of understanding them, because they are spiritually discerned *and* appreciated, [and he is unqualified to judge spiritual matters]. (1 Corinthians 2:14 AMP)

Going to the 144th floor not only represents elevation but acceleration, ascending 105 floors to get to the 144th floor from the 39th floor. Sometimes the numbers in our dreams point us to Scriptures. Ascending to the 144th floor pointed me to Psalm 144. Psalm 144:1–2 AMP states: "Blessed be the LORD, my Rock, and my great strength, Who trains my hand for war And my fingers for battle; My [steadfast] lovingkindness and my fortress, My high tower and my rescuer, My shield and He in whom I take refuge..." The Holy Spirit impressed upon me that the way my fingers fight and my hands war is through writing and publishing insight on the kingdom of God."

The man holding the glass of water is the Holy Spirit, the Teacher. When I encounter the Holy Spirit in my dreams, he usually appears as a professor. The glass of water represents the Word of God. The tea represents false teachings intermingled with the Word of God (water). The sweet tea had plastic ice cubes in it. The plastic ice cubes are reusable ice cubes that you freeze to make what you are drinking cold and not diluted with water. "Silica gel is a common ingredient in plastic and silicone ice cubes, which is toxic if it leaks into your beverage. While it holds a low toxicity level, it's still something you don't want to ingest, and it could damage your internal organs." The reusable ice cubes had melted into the hot sweet tea, making it toxic. When a person mixes the Word of God with false teachings instead of faith, it makes the Word of God ineffective in their life. "For indeed we have had the good news [of salvation] preached to us, just as the Israelites also [when the good news of the promised land came to them]; but the message they heard did not benefit them, because it was not united with faith [in God] by those who heard" (Hebrews 4:2 AMP).

When we are dreaming, we are engaging with the spiritual realm. As I transcended from the spiritual realm or dream realm to the natural realm, I held onto the memory of how the tea tasted—my mind could interpret what I was tasting in the dream realm as though I were continuing to taste it. The taste of the tea left a strong impression on my mind. "Just as my mouth can taste good food, so my mind tastes truth when I hear it" (Job 12:11 TLB).

The dish with the 1970s design represents an era. The woman represents the spirit of that age, the New Age Movement. In an article titled, "Religious Movement," J. Gordon Melton states the following: "New Age movement, movement that spread through the occult and metaphysical religious communities in the 1970s and '80s. It looked forward to a 'New age' of love and light and offered a foretaste of the coming era through personal transformation and healing."

The New Age movement embraces ideology that is contrary to the Bible. It can be very enticing to those who may not understand their spiritual identity or purpose. Transformation comes from spending time in the presence of God, studying the Bible, praying, and worshipping. Some have embraced a New Age teaching called Christ Consciousness. Christ Consciousness should not be confused with the idea that we should be Christ-like: loving, compassionate, and forgiving. We can only become like Christ through salvation and following the Word of God. An article titled "What Is the Christ Consciousness?" states the following:

> The Center for Christ Consciousness website defines Christ Consciousness as "the highest state of intellectual development and emotional maturity." They go on to claim that "Jesus achieved this [higher state of being] in his human life, and was given this

term [Christ] before his name as the recognition of his achievement of this spiritual status. This path is open to anyone regardless of their religious tradition if and when he or she is open to become a living vessel of love and truth on the planet and actively strives to attain..." It does not take much research to uncover the ancient roots of this idea. It is the same man-centered philosophy that is behind most religions.

In my dream, I was being elevated in my understanding of God's Word and how enticing New Age ideology can be. Unfortunately, some Christians have embraced New Age ideology to gain new insight. The Bible and New Age teachings are incompatible. Christ Consciousness teachings exemplify the embodiment of "false Christs" that Jesus told us would come. We have to guard our hearts and be very discerning about the source and content of any spiritual information presented to us. "Then if anyone says to you, 'Look, here is the Christ (the Messiah, the Anointed)!' or, 'Look, *He is* there!' do not believe it; for false Christs and false prophets will arise, and they will provide signs and wonders to deceive, if [such a thing were] possible, even the elect [those God has chosen for Himself]. But be on your guard; I have told you everything in advance" (Mark 13:21–23 AMP).

In researching the New Age Movement's birth, I read about another movement of the 1960s, the Human Potential Movement. These movements are centered around self-sufficiency. As believers, our spiritual growth, development, and potential depend on our obedience to the Word of God. Like the New Age movement, the Human Potential Movement appears to be positive. Still, it is very deceptive in teaching that social problems can be solved by developing human potential and helping others develop their potential, devoid of God. Our need for God's divine intervention and guidance is not mentioned.

> The Human Potential Movement (HPM) arose out of the counterculture movement of the 1960s and formed around the concept of cultivating extraordinary potential that its advocates believe to lie largely untapped in all people. The movement took as its premise the belief that through the development of quality of life filled with happiness, creativity, and fulfillment. As a corollary, those who begin to unleash this assumed potential often find themselves directing their actions within society towards assisting others to release their potential…

The gift of discerning of spirits was illustrated in interpreting this dream. It allowed me to identify the man holding the glass of water as the Holy Spirit, the Teacher, and the woman holding the iced tea as the spirit of the New Age Movement. According to the study course series, *The Holy Spirit and His Gifts*, "The discerning of spirits gives supernatural insight into the spiritual realm, "to discern" means to perceive by seeing or hearing. Therefore, discerning of spirits is the same as seeing or hearing in the realm of spirits."

Pray and ask not just for the interpretation of a dream but the purpose of a dream. I have seen people who are excellent Bible teachers embrace

New Age ideology. When I began to analyze this dream, I realized the Lord had given me the assignment to pray not just for those in the world who have embraced New Age ideology but for those who have left the church to pursue New Age teachings. I felt compelled to pray for grace and compassion for those who have embraced New Age teachings to receive salvation. I also felt compelled to pray for those who have renounced their faith in God to be restored.

When the Lord releases revelation to you, whether in a dream or waking hours, you become responsible for the information. We must be good stewards even over the revelation imparted to us in our dreams. Often, I have heard stewardship discussed concerning finances, but stewardship can apply to anything of value. "A biblical world view of stewardship can be consciously defined as: Utilizing and managing all resources God provides for the glory of God and the betterment of His creation. The central essence of biblical world view stewardship is managing everything God brings into the believer's life in a manner that honors God and impacts eternity."

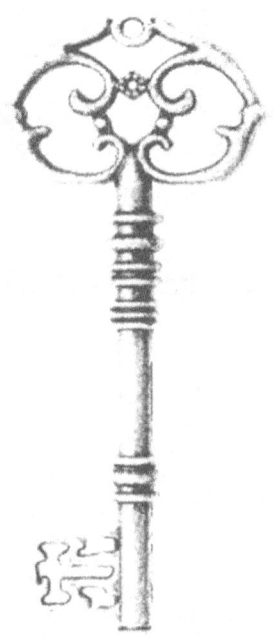

CHAPTER 18
UNLOCKING YOUR DESTINY

Dreams can release revelatory knowledge to unlock your destiny. The *King James Bible Dictionary* defines destiny as "state or condition appointed or predetermined; ultimate fate; as, men, are solicitous to know their future destiny which is however happily concealed from them." *Merriam Webster's Dictionary* defines destiny as "a power that is believed to control what happens in the future." Unlocking your destiny involves understanding God's plan, purpose, and assignments for your life. Understanding your identity is also a part of unlocking your destiny. "And we know [with great confidence] that God [who is deeply concerned about us] causes all things to work together [as a plan] for good for those who love God, to those who are called according to His plan and purpose. For those whom He foreknew [and loved and chose beforehand], He also predestined to be conformed to the image of His Son…" (Romans 8:28–29 AMP).

KEYS THAT UNLOCK DESTINY

I had a dream that I was driving, and my mother was the passenger in the front seat. A car had its door open, and to avoid a collision, I had to pass on the right side of the vehicle. I continued to drive down the road right off a cliff. I said to my mother, "I guess we're not going to get out of this one." The car landed safely and rolled up behind a bus. I thought we would collide with it, but the bus moved forward. I then realized I should have gotten onto the bus. I got on the next bus instead, and a stranger said to me, "Give me my keys." I reached into my left-hand pocket with my left hand and gave him many keys on a key ring.

ANALYSIS AND INTERPRETATION OF THE DREAM

My mother represents wisdom and my traveling companion. The car represents a traveling ministry directed by the Holy Spirit. Though I was sitting in the driver's seat, I was not in control of the car. The Holy Spirit was in control of the vehicle.

An open door can represent an opportunity. The car with the open door represents a ministerial opportunity, an invitation to teach or minister in a place. We have to know the will of God when we are sent out to minister; every ministry opportunity presented to us is not for us. If we accept the wrong opportunities, it can have disastrous results. They are designed to delay us from reaching our predestined places and fulfilling our assignments.

As we were falling off the cliff, I had peace, which signified my trust in God, even in times of uncertainty. When the car went off the cliff, it felt like we were floating through the air. We landed safely on the ground and avoided a second collision with the bus. The potential collisions represent obstacles I will encounter; however, the Holy Spirit will guide me in completing my assignments as I continue to trust and obey Him. "Trust in and rely confidently on the Lord with all your heart And do not rely on your own insight or understanding. In all your ways know and acknowledge and recognize Him, and He will make your paths straight and smooth [removing obstacles that block your way]" (Proverbs 3:5–6 AMP).

The bus I got on looked like a tour bus with large picture windows carrying us to our destinations. Getting to a destination represents reaching one's destiny. I was unaware that I had keys for a fellow traveler on the bus until he said, "Give me my keys." Having keys that belonged to another person represents, I can help people unlock their destiny. Reaching into my left-hand pocket with my left hand is significant because I am right-handed; I would not place my keys in my left pocket. What does the Bible say about the left hand? "Happy [blessed, considered fortunate, to be admired] is the man who finds [skillful and godly] *wisdom*, And the man who gains *understanding* and insight [learning from God's word and life's experiences], For wisdom's profit is better than the profit of silver, And her gain is better than fine gold. She is more precious than rubies; And nothing you can wish for compares with her [in value]. Long life is in her right hand; In her *left hand* are riches and honor" (Proverbs 3:13–16 AMP, emphasis added).

In my dream, the man was not only given authority to unlock his destiny but wisdom and resources to navigate the path leading to his destiny. When we understand how to use the keys or authority given to us, we can help others unlock their destiny. Understanding our assignment is an important part of helping others to understand theirs. This dream is an illustration of a word of wisdom (reveals the plan and purpose of God). I received this word of wisdom many years later, on August 8, 2018. I was told, "This is a season that the glory of the Lord is rising on you. I see God manifesting His dominion power. God says, 'I am resting on you to unlock destiny and fulfillment in the lives of my people. This is a time you will see a demonstration of my power. God says I will use you to destroy the plans of the enemy.'"

RIGHTLY DIVIDING THE WORD OF GOD

Over the years, I have prayed and believed God for a spirit of understanding to teach the Bible skillfully. One day, I was listening to a Sunday service message that disturbed me. In the service, I quietly prayed, "God give me an anointing to rightly divide your Word." Holy Spirit led me back to the Scripture 2 Timothy 2:15, "Study to shew thyself approved unto God, a workman that needeth not to be ashamed, rightly dividing the word of truth." I read this Scripture, and Holy Spirit said, "If you want an anointing to rightly divide the Word of God, then you will have to study."

THE DREAM

I had a dream that my youngest sister and I were in a large building and were getting ready to serve ribs. We were standing in front of a knife block with different knives. I was looking for the correct knife to cut the ribs properly. Once I had cut the ribs, which had no sauce, I placed them onto a silver tray. I began to serve a large group of people the ribs; then I woke up.

ANALYSIS AND INTERPRETATION OF THE DREAM

The ribs represent the Word of God. The ribs having no sauce meant teaching the Word of God without sugar-coating it; sugar coating means "to make superficially attractive or palatable." Also, *The KJV Dictionary* defines meat as the following:

1. In Scripture, spiritual food; that which sustains and nourishes spiritual life or holiness.

2. The more abstruse doctrines of the gospel, or mysteries of religion. Hebrews 5.

When I was Looking for the right knife to cut and separate the meat, it represented rightly dividing the Word of God or interpreting and teaching the Scriptures accurately. "Study *and* do your best to present yourself to God approved, a workman [tested by trial] who has no reason to be ashamed, accurately handling *and* skillfully teaching the word of truth" (2 Timothy 2:15 AMP).

The people being served the ribs were Muslims; It is forbidden for them to eat pork in observation of their religious beliefs, yet they were receiving the pork ribs in my dream. So, I knew that this meant the Holy Spirit had prepared the people's hearts to receive the gospel of the kingdom. The people receiving the meat signified that they were disciplined. The people were going to receive training to teach others to carry the gospel of the kingdom to their people and other nations.

Holy Spirit used this dream to reveal that He would send me overseas to teach the gospel of the kingdom. This dream illustrates a word of knowledge given to me: "You are a teacher of teachers." According to the study course series, *The Holy Spirit and His Gifts*, the word of knowledge is classified as one of the three revelatory gifts that release revelation or revelatory knowledge. The other two gifts are prophecy and the word of wisdom. "The word of knowledge is the supernatural revelation by the Holy Ghost of certain facts in the mind of God." Though we have seen social media become inundated with prophecies and people desiring prophecies over the Word of God, we will see many who have been called to the office of a teacher begin to arise. They will equip, train, and teach others how to develop the necessary skill sets to reach communities globally with the gospel of the kingdom.

DREAMS AND VISIONS

Throughout the Bible, dreams and visions have been used to unlock the identity and destiny of people called to bring transformation to systems and nations. When God reveals His secrets, a door to wisdom and revelation opens to increase your spiritual and intellectual capacity. Dreams are not only a gateway to understanding mysteries but are an invitation to become intimate with the Creator. As you continue to immerse yourself in studying the Word of God, dreams, and visions, you will birth innovative ideas and solutions to systemic problems. These divine plans will bring transformation to families and communities globally. As a citizen of the kingdom of God you have been given a mantle and keys—access to heavenly realms that contain wisdom and revelation to make a lasting impact on the world.

Use your keys!

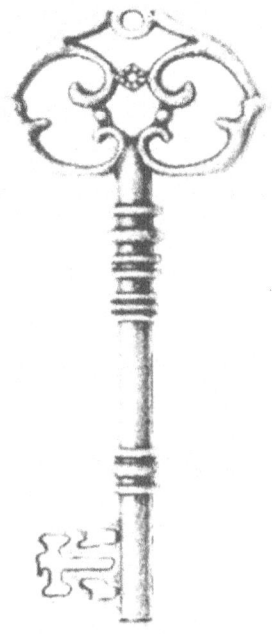

NOTES

INTRODUCTION

1. King James Bible Dictionary - Reference List –Discernment" 2021. *King James Bible Dictionary.* http://www.Kingjamesbibledictionary.com/Dictionary/discernment.

2. Unger, Merrill F, and William White, JR.1996. *Vines Complete Expository Dictionary Of Old And New Testament Words - With Topical Index.* Nashville: Thomas Nelson. "Definition of A Mystery, 424.

3. "Strong's Hebrew: 5197. (Nataph)—To Drop, Drip, Discourse". *Biblehub.Com*, 2020. https://biblehub.com/hebrew/ 5197.htm.
4. "Definition Of Insight | Dictionary.Com". 2022. *Www.Dictionary.Com*. https://www.dictionary.com/browse/insight.
5. Price, Paula A. 2006. *The Prophet's Dictionary: The Ultimate Guide To Supernatural Wisdom*. 3rd ed. New Kensington: Whitacker house, 303.
6. Riddle – Wikipedia". 2022. *En.Wikipedia.Org*. https://en.Wikipedia.org/wiki/Riddle.
7. Slick, Matt. 2014. "What Is Casting Lots? It Was A Method Used To Determine The Will Of God". Christian Apologetics & Research *Ministry*. https://carm.org/other-questions/ what-is-casting-lots/.
8. "OCCULT Definition".2021. *Biblestudy.Org*. https:// www. Biblestudy.org/beginner/definition-of-christian-terms/occult. html.

PART I: DREAMS, PATTERNS AND BLUEPRINTS
CHAPTER 1
DREAMS, SOLUTIONS, AND STRATEGIES

1. Hagin, Kenneth. *The Holy Spirit And His Gifts*, Tulsa: Tulsa, 102.
2. Stratos, Anita. "Egypt: Perchance To: Dreams And Their Meaning In Ancient Egypt Dream". *Tour egypt.Net*, 2020. http://www.Tour egypt.net /featurestories/dream. htm#:~: text=Thousands %20 of %20 years%20ago%2 C%20 ancient, divine%20 predictions %20of%20 the %20future.

CHAPTER 2
HEAVENLY PATTERNS

1. "Definition Of Wisdom". 2022. *Merriam-Webster.* https://www.merriam-webster.com/ dictionary/wisdom.
2. "Definition Of Understanding". 2022. *Merriam-Webster.* https://www.merriam-webster.com/ dictionary/ understanding.
3. *Webster's New World Dictionary of The American Language. College Edition.* 1954. USA: The World Publishing Company, 215.

CHAPTER 3
WORSHIP, THE KEY TO WISDOM

1. Conner, Kevin J. 1986. *The tabernacle of David.* Portland, Ore.: City Bible Pub, 152.
2. Tikanen, Amy. 2020. "Ark Of The Covenant Religion". *Encyclopedia* Britannica. https://www.britannica.com/topic/Ark-of-the-Covenant.

CHAPTER 4
CLOTHED IN HUMILITY

1. Unger, Merrill F, and William White, JR. 1996. *Vines Complete Expository Dictionary Of Old And New Testament Words - With Topical Index.* Nashville: Thomas Nelson. "Definition of Repent, 525.
2. Deal, Ron. 2019. "With Humility Comes Wisdom (Proverbs 11)| Family Life Blended®". *Family life blended.Com.* http://family life blended.com/program/with-humility-comes-wisdom-proverbs-11/.

3. "CLOTHE - Definition From The KJV Dictionary". 2020. *AV 1611.Com.* https://av1611.com/kjbp/kjv-dictionary/cloth.html.

CHAPTER 5
MYSTERY OF WISDOM

1. "King James Bible Dictionary - Reference List Invention". 2019. *King James Bible Dictionary.* http://kingjamesbible dictionary .com / Dictionary / proverb.
2. "Definition Of Witty". 2022. *Merriam-Webster.* https://www.merriam-webster.com/dictionary/witty.
3. "King James Bible Dictionary - Reference List Invention". 2019. *King James Bible Dictionary.* http://kingjamesbible dictionary .com /Dictionary/ invention.
4. Unger and White, *Vines Complete Expository Dictionary* "Definition of The Heart, 109.

CHAPTER 6
A TYPE OF THE KING AND HIS KINGDOM

1. "What Is The Significance Of Biblical Typology? - Christian Research Institute". n.d. http://www.equip.org/bible answers/what-is-the-significance-of-biblical-typology/
2. Unger and White, *Vines Complete Expository Dictionary,* "Definition of Rod, 537.
3. Unger and White, *Vines Complete Expository Dictionary,* "Definition of Root, 539.

CHAPTER 7
GUARD YOUR HEART

1. Hayford, Jack. 2017. *Majesty*. [S.l.]: Gateway Create Pub.
2. "IDOLATRY - Definition From The KJV Dictionary". 2020. *AV1611.Com*. https://av1611.com/kjbp/kjv-dictionary/idolatry.html.

PART II: DREAMS AND TRANSFORMATION OF THE MIND
CHAPTER 8
DREAMS AND REVELATORY KNOWLEDGE

1. "Revelation". 2021. *Dictionary.Cambridge.Org*. https://dictionary.cambridge.org/us/dictionary/english/revelation.
2. Levine, John. 2022. "Conformity | Definition, Studies, Types, & Facts". *Encyclopedia Britannica*. https://www.britannica.com/topic/conformity.
3. 2021. *Fire of the lord ministries.Org*. http://fireofthelordministries.org/nav/Color%20Interpretation%20Chart.pdf.
4. Unger and White, *Vines Complete Expository Dictionary* "Definition of Veil, 658.
5. Hagin, *The Holy Spirit And His Gifts*, 154.

CHAPTER 9
SYSTEMS

1. *The Matrix*. 1999. Film. Sydney, Australia: Fox Studios.
2. "A Quote By Thomas Jefferson". 2022. *Goodreads.Com*. https://www.goodreads.com/quotes/1361034-if-you-want-something-you-ve-never-had-you-must-be.

3. "Oliver Wendell Holmes: One's Mind, Once stretched by a New Idea, Never Regains Its Original Dimensions.".2018. *Quotes.Net*. https://www.quotes.net/quote/4003.

CHAPTER 10
TECHNOLOGY AND SPIRITUAL CAPACITY

1. Dr. Cindy Trimm. *How To Engage The Anointing To Be An Overcomer*. 2017. Video. YouTube: The Gospel 4U.
2. "What Is RAM (Random Access Memory)?". 2018. *Lifewire*. https://www.lifewire.com/what-is-random-access-memory-ram-2618159.
3. US, Dell 2018. "How Random Access Memory (RAM) Affects Performance | Dell UK".*Dell.Com*. http://www.dell.com/support/article/us/en/04/sln179266/how-random-access-memory-ramaffectsperformance?lang=en.

    Understanding RAM Generally, the more RAM your system has, the larger the digital countertop you have to work on and the faster your programs will run. If your system is running slowly due to lack of RAM, you might be tempted to increase virtual memory because it's less expensive. However, adding RAM is a better solution because your processor can read data from RAM. RAM has two main attributes that affect your system's performance: memory capacity and memory speed.

4. "Definition Of Paradigm Shift". 2022. *Merriam-Webster*. https://www.merriam-webster.com/dictionary/paradigm%20shift

5. "Definition Of Paradigm". 2022. *Merriam-Webster*. https:// www.merriam-webster.com/ dictionary/paradigm.

CHAPTER 11
DOORS IN YOUR MIND

1. "Mind | Definition Of Mind In English By Oxford Dictionaries". 2019. *OxfordDictionaries|English*.https://en.Oxford dictionaries. com/definition/mind
2. Dr. Cindy Trimm. *How to Engage The Anointing to Be An Overcomer*. 2017. Video. YouTube: The Gospel 4U.
3. "Subconscious". 2022. *Dictionary.Cambridge.Org*. https://dictionary. cambridge.org/us/dictionary/english/subconscious.
4. "Edgar Allan Poe Society Of Baltimore - Works - Rejected - An Opinion On Dreams [Text-02]". 2021. *Eapoe.Org*. https:// www. eapoe.org/works/rejected/opindrms.htm.
5. "Definition Of Imagery". 2022. *Merriam-Webster*. https://www. merriam-webster. com/ dictionary/imagery.
6. "Hebrew Roots /Neglected Commandments/Idolatry/Sunday– Wikibooks, Open Books For An Open World". 2021. En. M. Wikibooks.Org.https://en.m.wikibooks.org/wiki/Hebrew_Roots/ Neglected_Commandments/Idolatry/Sunday.

CHAPTER 12
AWAKENING TO UNDERSTANDING

1. "Sleep and Cell Regeneration". 2018. *DHM Health Research*. http:// www.dailyhealthmagazine.com/sleep-and-the-cell-regeneration-process/.

2. Green, Ethan. 2020. "False Awakening: Dreaming About Waking Up". *No Sleepless Nights*. https://www.Nosleepless nights.com/false-awakening/.
3. DiGiulio, Sarah. 2017. "What Actually Happens In Your Body And Brain While You Sleep". *NBC News*. https://www.nbcnews.com/better/health/what-happens-your-body-brain-while-you-sleep-ncna805276.
4. "1989 Oldmobile New Generation Tv Commercial – Youtube". 2020. *Youtube.Com*. https://www.youtube.com/ results? search_query= 1989 +oldmobile+new+generation+tv+ commercial.
5. Thompson, Beale, and King, *The Divinity Code*, 404.

PART III: THE KEYS

CHAPTER 13
THE KEYS OF THE KINGDOM

1. "Key. - Smith's Bible Dictionary Online". 2021.Biblestudytools. Com.https://www.biblestudytools.com/dictionaries/smiths-bible-dictionary/key.html.
2. "Definition Of Charge". 2022. https://www.merriam-webster.com/dictionary/charge.
3. "SHOULDER - Definition From The KJV Dictionary". 2021. AV1611.Com.https://av1611.com/kjbp/kjv-dictionary/shoulder.html.
4. "Matthew 16:19 Commentaries: "I Will Give You The Keys Of The Kingdom Of Heaven; And Whatever You Bind On Earth Shall Have Been Bound In Heaven, And Whatever You Loose On

Earth Shall Have Been Loosed In Heaven." ".2021. Biblehub.Com. https:// biblehub. com/commentaries/ matthew /16-19.htm.

5. Eckhardt, John. 2011. *The Invisible King and His Kingdom*. Mary, Fla.: Charisma House, 127.

6. "Luke 11:52 Commentaries: "Woe To You Lawyers! For You Have Taken Away The Key of Knowledge; You Yourselves Did Not Enter, and You Hindered Those Who Were Entering." ".2018. *Biblehub*.com. http://biblehub.com/commentaries/luke/11-52.htm

7. Price, *The Prophet's Dictionary*, 373.

8. "A Quote By Horace Greeley". 2022. *Goodreads.Com*. https://www.goodreads.com/quotes/117998-it-is-impossible-to-enslave-mentally-or-socially-a-bible-reading.

9. Index, Content, and Books Bible. 2021. "What Is The Key Of David? | Gotquestions.Org". *Gotquestions.Org*. https://www.gotquestions.org /key-of-David.html.

10. The Key of David. Org. http://www.The keyofdavid.org

CHAPTER 14
SPIRITUAL IDENTITY

1. "God In America - People - Harriet Tubman". 2010. *God In America*.https://www.pbs.org/wgbh/pages/frontline/godinamerica/people/harriettubman.html.ages/frontline/godinamerica/people/harriet-tubman.html

CHAPTER 15
REVELATORY KEYS AND MYSTERIES

1. 2021. *Raised praise banner.Com*. https://www.raisedpraise banners.com/biblical-color-meaning.
2. "WORD STUDY – TREASURES OF DARKNESS | Chaim Bentorah". 2021. *Chaimbentorah.Com*. https://www.chaimbentorah.com/2014/01/word-study-treasures-darkness/.

CHAPTER 16
MANTLES

1. Thompson, Beale, and King, *The Divinity Code*, 232.
2. Studies, Unique, and Meaning Bible. 2022. "Meaning Of The Number 25 In The Bible". *Biblestudy.Org*. https://www.biblestudy.org/bibleref/meaning-of-numbers-in-bible/25.html.

CHAPTER 17
UNLOCKING YOUR UNDERSTANDING

1. Price, *The Prophet's Dictionary*, 53.
2. "LIGHT - Definition From The KJV Dictionary". 2021. *AV 1611.Com*. https://av1611.com/kjbp/kjv-dictionary/light.html.
3. "Definition Of Barrier | Dictionary.Com". 2022. *Www.Dictionary.Com*. https://www.dictionary.com/browse/barrier.
4. "Definition Of Breakthrough | Dictionary.Com". 2022. *Www.Dictionary.Com*. https:// www.dictionary.com/ browse/breakthrough.

5. Gordon, Melton J. 2022. "New Age Movement | Religious Movement". *Encyclopedia Britannica*. https://www.britannica.com/topic/New-Age-movement.
6. "What's In Plastic Ice Cubes – Bing". *Bing.Com*, 2020. https://www.bing.com/search?q=whats+in+plastic+ice+cubes&for=ANSPH1&refig=4e308b4bb1da45d7804456a6b79d400f.
7. Practices. "What Is The Christ Consciousness? | Gotquestions.Org". *Gotquestions.Org*, 2020. https://www.Gotquestions.org/Christ-consciousness.html.
8. "Stewardship (Theology)". En.Wikipedia.Org, 2020. https://en.wikipedia.org/wiki/Stewardship_(theology)#:~:text=A%20biblical%20world%20view%20of,a%20manner%20that%20honors%20God.
9. "Human Potential Movement". *En Wikepedia.Org*, 2020. https://en.wikipedia.org/wiki/Human_Potential_Movement#:~:text=The%20Human%20Potential%20Movement%20(HPM,largely%20untapped%20in%20all%20people.
10. "Counterculture Of The 1960S". *En.Wikipedia.Org*, 2020. https://en.wikipedia.org/wiki/Counterculture_of_the_1960s.
11. Hagin, *The Holy Spirit And His Gifts*, 109.

CHAPTER 18
UNLOCKING YOUR DESTINY

1. "King James Bible Dictionary - Reference List – Destiny". 2022. *King James Bible Dictionary*. https://kingjamesbibledictionary.com/Dictionary/destiny.

2. Hagin, *The Holy Spirit And His Gifts*, 85.
3. "Definition Of Sugarcoat". 2022. *Merriam-Websters*. https://www.merriam-webster.com/dictionary/sugarcoat.
4. "MEAT - Definition From The KJV Dictionary". 2020. *AV1611.Com*. https://av1611.com/kjbp/kjv-dictionary/meat.html.

www.ingramcontent.com/pod-product-compliance
Lightning Source LLC
Chambersburg PA
CBHW062038120526
44592CB00035B/1242

www.ingramcontent.com/pod-product-compliance

Lightning Source LLC
Chambersburg PA
CBHW062035120526
4492CB00036B/2135